RE-SET THE MIND

&

Adjust Your Thinking

Neuroscience and The Bible

Harrison S. Mungal, Ph.D, Psy.D

RESET THE MIND & ADJUST YOUR THINKING

Unless otherwise identified, Scripture quotations are from

New King James Version of the Bible.

Contact author via email:
hsmungal@hotmail.com
info@agetoage.ca
www.agetoage.ca
www.harrisonmungal.com
Facebook: Harrison Mungal
Twitter: AgeToAgeInc1
LinkedIn: Harrison Mungal, Ph.D., PsyD
YouTube: Harrison Mungal
Phone: 905-533-1334

ABOUT *the* AUTHOR

Harrison Mungal, PhD, PsyD

Dr. Mungal has two doctoral degrees, one in Clinical Psychology and the other in Philosophy in Social Work, dual master's degrees in Social Work and Christian Counselling, and a Bachelor degree in Theology. He worked over 20 years in the fields of mental health and psychiatry then went into psychology. He worked with people from a wide range of backgrounds, including brain injury survivors, refugees, victims of war, PTSD victims, those struggling with mental health and in crisis. He liaison with police, hospitals, community agencies, and inpatient mental health settings.

Dr. Mungal is completely dedicated to improving the lives of his clients. He is known all over the world in over 47 nations for his deep knowledge of neuroscience, mental health, biblical studies and topics supporting individuals, couples and families and businesses.

Dr. Mungal is a highly sought-after workshop presenter who uses his practical approach to help understand the functionality of psychology and spirituality. His global impact is clear from the way he uses humour and enthusiasm to make complicated talks about mental health, addiction, relationships, and parenting at conferences, seminars, and media platforms.

Dr. Mungal's new and scientifically sound methods have been praised by many institutions, earning him awards and recogniztions. He spreads his influence by training and advising a wide range of community partners, such as respected professionals in the fields of medicine, social work, first responders, law enforcement, and senior management teams.

Dr. Mungal is a leader in cutting-edge cognitive research that looks at mental health issues like addiction, psychosis, anxiety, and depression. His work includes research on music therapy and schizophrenia, substance abuse and addictions in the food service industry, and vaccination for children under six years old.

Dr. Mungal practical therapeutic toolbox includes evidence-based therapies including Cognitive Behavioural Therapy (CBT), Cognitive Processing Therapy (CPT), Dialectical Behavioural Therapy (DBT), Thought Developmental Practice (TDP), Acceptance and Commitment Therapy (ACT). Interpersonal therapy (IPT), Motivational Interviewing Techniques, Grounding Techniques, Integrative Eclectic Therapy, Humanistic Experiential Therapy, Interpersonal Therapy, Supportive Therapy, Exposure Therapy, Visual Therapy, Psychodynamic Therapy.

TABLE *Of* CONTENT

INTRODUCTION

This book "*Reset You Brain and Adjust You Thinking*" is a real plea for you to start over in your mind, heart, and soul. It's for people who have ever felt like they were stuck in a cycle of bad thoughts, too busy with life, or like they didn't know what to do. I wrote it because I've been through burnout, anxiety, and spiritual dryness. You can't heal on your own, which is what I learned on my journey. When we learn how our brains work, line up our thoughts with the truth, and let God change us from the inside out, we can change.

The point of this book is to help people begin a journey of spiritual, mental, and emotional renewal. It's for people who are really stressed out, can't stop having bad thoughts, or don't know what their inner peace and purpose are. "*Reset You Brain and Adjust You Thinking*" is a helpful and kind guide to healing if you're burned out, anxious, or just want to see things more clearly. It uses both neuroscience and biblical wisdom to show that change is not only possible, but also strongly supported by both science and scripture.

Readers will learn how stress and emotional exhaustion over time affect the brain, and how spiritual renewal can help them feel better and see things more clearly. People talk a lot about neuroplasticity, which is the brain's ability to change the way it is wired. People can think that change is not just a dream, but a fact of life. This book shows you how to stop thinking negatively and start thinking positively, which will help you live a better life. It does this by using ideas from cognitive psychology and the Bible. It talks about how hard it is to change when you're competitive and how spiritual discipline and doing things on purpose over and over can help you stick to new habits.

"Reset You Brain and Adjust You Thinking" teaches you how to get your focus and mental clarity back in a world full of digital distractions. It does this by being quiet, spending time outside, and thinking about spiritual things. It shows how important sleep, nutrition, and movement are and how small changes to your daily routine can have big effects on your mental health. Mindfulness and meditation teach readers how to deal with their emotions and connect with their spiritual side. These practices use both psychological methods and biblical meditation to help people feel calm and present.

This book tells people to be willing to try new things and be open to them. It also talks about how trying new things can help the brain grow and heal emotionally. It helps them let go of feelings of guilt, shame, and fear and accept grace, truth, and forgiveness. Silence is not shown as emptiness; instead, it is shown as a powerful tool for healing that can calm the nervous system and help people connect with God.

This book shows how both psychology and the Bible can help people who are burned out feel better. This will help them get their energy back and find out what they want to do with their lives again. It is good for both your body and your mind to move around. It can make you feel better and more open-minded. They help people change their negative thoughts and make their mental patterns match spiritual truth by showing them how thoughts and feelings are connected. Readers learn how to be strong and love learning for the rest of their lives. They also learn what it means to have a fixed or growth mindset.

"Reset You Brain and Adjust You Thinking" talks about cognitive biases so that readers can see and change the wrong mental shortcuts that make it hard for them to think clearly and with empathy. People don't think of failure as the end; they think of it as a chance to learn and get better. You can learn from your mistakes and make them better.

Mental agility is a skill that helps you change and act wisely. Doing exercises to improve your emotional control and flexibility can help. This book shows you how to change your thinking from reactive to reflective. This means that you should take your time when you respond quickly so that you can be wise and graceful. It talks about how important it is to let go of old thoughts and feelings so that you can make room for new ones.

It's better to be curious than to judge because curiosity helps people get along and understand each other better. We teach systems thinking so that people can see the big picture and make better decisions.

Finally, this book talks about how spiritual practices and therapy can help you deal with and heal painful memories. Readers can rewrite their own stories in a way that is honest and kind. This book is more than just a list of facts; it's a call to clear your mind, lift your spirits, and find the joy of living with purpose and clarity again.

This book is educational and useful. It uses both science and faith to help you become the person you were meant to be.

"Reset You Brain and Adjust You Thinking" isn't just a collection of chapters; it's a trip. A trip that leads to healing, understanding, and growth. This is a helpful book that uses both science and faith to help you become the person you were meant to be. As you read this, I hope you feel seen, supported, and motivated to start over.

RE-SET THE BRAIN

MENTAL RENEWAL

During my recent journey to Bali, Indonesia, in October 2023, I experienced what I can only describe as a profound "brain reset." Kathleen and I had first traveled together to Dubai, and while she returned to Canada, I continued on to Bali before heading to the Philippines for a medical conference with fellow doctors. That time alone—especially by the beach, watching the sun melt into the horizon—gave me the space to be still. In that quiet, I spent time with God, reflecting deeply on what truly matters, not just for myself, but for my family.

I began my professional journey in 1987 after migrating to Canada. My early years were spent working on a farm, followed by hands-on roles as a drywall taper and later in group homes supporting individuals with developmental delays and acquired brain injuries. These formative experiences laid the groundwork for my deep commitment to human service and mental health.

Driven by a calling to serve, I pursued theological studies at Bible college and from 1994 to 1997, served as a missionary in Croatia—years marked by profound experiences and traumas that continue to shape my empathy and clinical insight. Together with my wife Kathleen, we were blessed with seven children. We planted two churches, pastored in four congregations and lead a Bible college for ten years.

My academic path continued with a return to university, where I earned two master's degrees—one in Christian Counselling and one in Social Work—and two doctoral degrees in Clinical Psychology and Philosophy in Social Work. Throughout this time, I balanced multiple roles, often working across three jobs simultaneously.

Eventually, I transitioned into private practice, where I provided psychotherapy to an average of 35 to 40 clients per week, after working seventeen years in mental health. My clinical focus has included trauma recovery, family systems, addiction treatment, and emotional regulation. Each client's story has deepened my understanding of resilience and the human capacity for healing. This journey has not only shaped my professional identity but also reaffirmed my belief that transformation is possible—no matter how complex the past.

Somewhere along the way, I began to feel the weight of it all. The burnout crept in quietly, and I found myself asking: what is the end result of this constant striving? That moment in Bali helped me answer that question. My reset was about realigning my priorities—making Kathleen and I the center again, and embracing our children, grandchildren, parents, siblings, friends, and work with a sense of balance rather than burden.

This shift lifted nearly 80-90% of the emotional weight I had been carrying—the belief that I had to stay busy, fix everyone's problems, say yes to everything, and be liked by everyone. That mindset had kept me trapped in a cycle of exhaustion. But in Bali, I let go. That reset didn't just lighten my load—it set me free. It brought clarity, peace, and a significant reduction in stress. I returned not just rested, but renewed.

Before this reset, there was a morning I'll never forget. I was sitting at my kitchen table, staring into a half-empty coffee mug, watching the steam curl upward like a question mark. My mind felt like a cluttered attic — dusty, disorganized, full of things I hadn't looked at in years. Thoughts raced, but none of them felt useful. I was overwhelmed, exhausted, and strangely numb. That was the moment I realized: I needed to reset my brain.

Not just rest. Not just a vacation. I needed a full-on reboot — the kind you give a computer when it's frozen and nothing works. I didn't know how to do it yet, but I knew something had to change.

Mental fog doesn't arrive like a thunderstorm. It creeps in slowly, like mist over a lake. You don't notice it at first — the missed appointments, the short temper, the inability to focus. You chalk it up to being busy, to aging, to stress. But eventually, you realize you're not thinking clearly. You're reacting instead of responding. You're surviving instead of living.

For me, it started with burnout. I was juggling work, family, and a dozen other responsibilities. I prided myself on being productive, on getting things done. But somewhere along the way, I stopped feeling joy. I was tired all the time. I couldn't remember the last time I laughed — really laughed — from my belly. And, to top it off, I had a young man hang himself in my unit I was working at. He was only 23 years old.

One afternoon, I snapped at one of my daughters; I have six daughters and one son. She was spilling juice on the floor. She looked up at me, eyes wide, and said, "It's just juice, Dad." That moment broke me. I wasn't angry about the juice. I was angry because my brain was overloaded. I was angry because I hadn't taken care of myself.

Resetting the brain starts with permission. Permission to stop. To breathe. To not be productive for a moment. That's harder than it sounds. We live in a culture that worships hustle. Rest is seen as weakness. But the truth is, rest is revolutionary.

I started small. I gave myself 10 minutes a day to sit in silence. No phone. No music. Just me and my breath. At first, it was uncomfortable. My mind rebelled. It threw thoughts at me like darts — to-do lists, regrets, worries. But slowly, the noise began to fade. I began to hear something quieter underneath: my own voice.

One of the most powerful ways to reset the brain is through novelty. New experiences light up dormant parts of the brain. They shake us out of autopilot. I remember signing up for a dance class with Kathleen. We had never danced before, and she was seven months pregnant. We were terrible at it — we looked like kids dancing in the rain. But we laughed. We felt alive. We were learning again.

That's the thing about novelty — it doesn't have to be grand. It can be as simple as taking a different route to work, trying a new recipe, or listening to music from a genre you've never explored. Each new experience is a spark. And enough sparks can reignite a fire.

I used to think exercise was about losing weight. Now I know it's about gaining clarity. When I started walking every morning, especially during covid-19 — just 20 minutes around the block — something shifted. My thoughts became less tangled. My mood lifted. I felt more present.

There's something magical about moving your body. It's like shaking a snow globe. The chaos settles. You see things more clearly. And it doesn't have to be intense. Dance in your kitchen. Stretch on your living room floor. Just move.

Let's talk about screens. I love technology. I'm grateful for it. But it was hijacking my brain. I was checking my phone at lease 100 times a day. Scrolling endlessly. Consuming more than I was creating. My attention span was shrinking. My anxiety was growing.

I did something radical: I turned off notifications. I deleted social media apps for a week. I replaced screen time with writing books. An hour dedicated just to write. The first few days were hard. I felt phantom vibrations in my pocket. But then — silence. Glorious silence. My thoughts became my own again.

One of the most healing parts of resetting the brain is rediscovering joy. Not the kind that comes from achievement or praise. The quiet kind. The kind that bubbles up when you're watching birds at a feeder, or sipping tea in the sun, or laughing with a friend about something silly.

I started keeping a joy journal. Every night, I wrote down one thing that made me smile. Some days it was big — like watching my son score a goal in soccer. Other days it was small — like the smell of fresh basil. But over time, I trained my brain to look for joy. And it found it.

We carry so much in our minds — regrets, grudges, fears. They weigh us down. Part of resetting the brain is decluttering it. I remember writing a letter to someone I hadn't spoken to in years. I didn't send it. I just needed to say the words. To release the weight.

Forgiveness is a powerful reset. Not just for others — for ourselves. I had to forgive myself for the times I wasn't present. For the mistakes I made. For the ways I neglected my own needs. That forgiveness opened space. Space for healing. Space for growth.

I can't talk about resetting the brain without mentioning sleep. For years, I treated sleep like an inconvenience. I stayed up late, woke up early, and bragged about how little rest I needed. But sleep isn't optional. It's foundational. I worked shift work, and my sleep was disruptive.

When I started prioritizing sleep — going to bed at the same time, creating a calming bedtime routine, avoiding screens before bed —

everything changed. My memory improved. My mood stabilized. My creativity returned. Sleep is the brain's reset button.

There's a whisper inside all of us. It's quiet, but persistent. It tells us when something's off. When we're out of alignment. When we need to change. For years, I ignored that whisper. I drowned it out with busyness. But when I finally listened, it led me home.

Resetting the brain isn't a one-time event. It's a practice. A rhythm. A way of life. It's about tuning in, slowing down, and making space for what matters. It's about choosing presence over performance. Connection over consumption. Joy over judgment.

Start with one breath. One walk. One moment of silence. One act of kindness toward yourself. Your brain is resilient. It's waiting for you. And when you reset it — when you clear the clutter and reconnect with your essence — you'll remember who you are.

Not the roles you play. Not the tasks you complete. But the soul underneath. The one who laughs freely. Who loves deeply. Who dreams boldly.

There's something deeply humbling about realizing your mind needs help. Not because you're broken, but because you've been carrying too much for too long. I remember standing in the shower one morning, letting the water run over me, and thinking, "I don't know what I'm feeling anymore." The surface-level resets were helping, but my brain needed more than just a breather — it needed healing from the trauma of losing a patient, among other stressors.

I started creating that space for myself. I lit candles in the evening. I played music that soothed me. I wrote letters to myself — kind, forgiving letters. I stopped pushing away hard emotions and started sitting with them. Fear. Sadness. Loneliness. They weren't enemies. They were messengers. And when I listened, they softened.

One of the most unexpected tools in my reset journey was nature. I began spending time outside — not just walking, but noticing. I grew up in the bush, no running water or electricity. Forest bathing is fun. Getting lost in the forest is fun. The way the leaves changed colour. The sound of birds in the morning. The feel of grass under my feet. Nature doesn't rush. It doesn't multitask. It just is. And being in its presence reminded me that I could just be, too.

There was a day I sat under a tree in my front yard for an hour, doing nothing. No phone. No book. Just watching the wind move through the branches. I felt something shift inside me — a quiet joy, a sense of belonging. It was as if my brain had been waiting for me to slow down enough to hear its whisper.

I also began to pay attention to what I consumed — not just food, but information. I unfollowed accounts that made me feel inadequate. I stopped watching news that left me anxious. I chose books that nourished me. Podcasts that inspired me. Conversations that uplifted me. My brain was a garden, and I became intentional about what I planted.

One evening, I was journaling and wrote the words, "I am allowed to change." It hit me like a wave. So much of my mental clutter came from trying to stay the same — to meet expectations, to maintain identities, to hold onto routines that no longer served me. But change is not betrayal. It's growth. And giving myself permission to evolve was one of the most liberating resets of all.

I started saying no more often. Not out of defiance, but out of clarity. I said no to projects that drained me. To social events that felt obligatory. To habits that kept me stuck. And every no was a yes to something deeper — to rest, to creativity, to alignment.

Creativity, by the way, is a powerful brain reset. I began painting again — something I hadn't done since college. I wasn't good at it, but that didn't matter. The act of mixing colours, of making something out of nothing, was medicine. It reminded me that I could create beauty. That I could express without performing. That I could play.

Play is underrated. As adults, we forget how to play. We think it's childish, frivolous. But play is how we reconnect with joy, with spontaneity, with imagination. I started playing board games with my kids. Making up silly songs. Dancing in the living room. And each moment of play was a breath of fresh air for my tired brain.

I also learned to celebrate small wins. Not just the big milestones, but the quiet victories. Getting out of bed on a hard day. Saying something kind to myself. Choosing a nourishing meal. These moments mattered. They were proof that I was healing. That I was showing up for myself.

There was a night I couldn't sleep. My mind was racing. Instead of fighting it, I got up and sat by the window. The moon was full, casting a soft glow over the neighborhood. I watched it for a long time, and something inside me settled. I realized that resetting the brain isn't about erasing thoughts. It's about changing your relationship with them. About learning to observe without judgment. To breathe through the noise.

I began practicing gratitude — not as a checklist, but as a mindset. I started noticing what was good, even on hard days. The warmth of a blanket. The taste of coffee. The smile of a stranger. Gratitude rewired my brain. It shifted my focus from lack to abundance. From fear to trust.

And slowly, I began to feel like myself again. Not the version of me that was always busy, always achieving, always pleasing. But the version that was present. Grounded. Whole.

I still have foggy days. I still get overwhelmed. But now I have tools. I have rituals. I have awareness. I know when to pause. When to breathe. When to ask for help. I know how to reset.

You don't have to earn rest. You don't have to justify joy. You are allowed to feel, to change, to grow. You are allowed to reset.

And when you do — when you clear the clutter and reconnect with your essence — you'll find something beautiful waiting for you.

NEUROPLASTICITY

HOW YOUR BRAIN CAN REWIRE ITSELF?

I used to think that my mind was set. That the way I thought, reacted, and understood the world was mostly fixed. I thought my habits, emotional patterns, and mental wiring were all set in stone. But then I learned about neuroplasticity, which is the brain's amazing ability to change how it works. Everything changed after that.

Neuroplasticity is the scientific term for how the brain can change and adapt based on what you do, learn, and practice on purpose. It means that our brains are always changing. They change all the time. They can make new neural pathways, make connections stronger, and even heal from trauma. This truth sets me free and makes me feel small. And as I started to look into it, I couldn't help but see how it was similar to what the Bible says.

"Do not conform to the pattern of this world, but be transformed by the renewing of your mind," says Romans 12:2. That verse has always made me feel something.

But as I learned more about neuroplasticity, it became more meaningful to me. Paul wasn't just using metaphors. He was talking about a process that science now agrees with: change through renewal. Not just renewing the spirit, but also the mind. Changing the way you think. The rearranging of mental habits. The brain's wiring has changed.

This has happened to me before. For a long time, I had anxiety, which was always there and affected how I saw the world. I thought that was just how I was. But things started to change when I started to practice mindfulness, prayer, and replacing negative thoughts with positive ones. My brain started to work differently over time. The panic pathways got weaker. The paths to peace got stronger. It didn't happen right away. It was hard. But it was true.

Philippians 4:8 became my anchor: *"Whatever is true, whatever is noble, whatever is right... think about such things."* That verse isn't just a suggestion. It's a plan. It's a plan for changing the way your mind works. When we focus on truth, beauty, and goodness, we don't just feel better; we also change our brains. We're strengthening the neural pathways that help us feel joy, hope, and resilience.

Neuroplasticity also makes me think of God's grace. That He not only forgives our past but also gives us the strength to move forward. That He doesn't just heal our hearts; He also makes our minds new. God says in Ezekiel 36:26, *"I will give you a new heart and put a new spirit in you."* This promise also includes our mental health. The way we think. How we feel about things. Our ability to change.

I've noticed this in other people as well. A friend of mine had a lot of criticism in their home when they were growing up. His inner voice was mean and unyielding. But with the help of therapy, the Bible, and his friends, he started to question those thoughts. He started to tell the truth about himself. He started to change the way he thought. And over time, his mind changed. His inner voice got quieter. He got more sure of himself. He felt more at peace. That's how the brain changes. That's a new start.

Science says that doing the same thing over and over again makes neural connections stronger. That the more we do something, like be grateful, kind, or brave, the easier it gets. That's why spiritual practices are important. Prayer, worship, and reading the Bible are not just things you do. They are tools for rewiring. They change how we think. They shape our hearts. They help our brains understand what God says.

"*I have hidden your word in my heart so that I won't sin against you,*" says Psalm 119:11. That hiding isn't just sitting around. It is active. It's putting the truth into our brains every day. It's the deliberate shaping of our mental landscape.

Neuroplasticity gives me hope for getting better. The idea that the brain can change is revolutionary for people who have been through trauma, addiction, or deep emotional pain. It means that the past doesn't have to control what happens in the future. You can fix that brokenness. That new patterns can come up.

Jesus often healed people in more than one way. He healed them physically, mentally, and emotionally. He gave back dignity. He changed the stories. He got people to think in new ways. He made statements like, "*Go and sin no more.*" "*Your faith has made you well.*" "*Take heart.*" These weren't just words; they changed everything. They were ways to open up new neural pathways. To new identities. To new lives.

Neuroplasticity is not only a scientific idea; it's also a spiritual truth. It's how God made our brains. Able to change. Able to be renewed. And when we line that design up with His truth, things change.

If you've ever felt stuck in a habit, a way of thinking, or a pattern, I want you to know that change is possible. You can change how your brain works. Your mind can change. You can refresh your mind.

Start with a little. Tell the truth. Be graceful. Think about the good things. And have faith that the God who made your brain also made a way for it to get better.

You are not what you used to be. Your patterns do not define you. You are a soul that is alive, learning, and renewing. And your mind— strong, open, and healed—is ready to grow.

I thought my mind was set in stone, like a blueprint. I thought that the way I handled stress, the habits I had, and the thoughts I kept having were just part of who I was. I didn't ask them any questions. I didn't fight them. I just put up with them, even when they made me unhappy. But then things changed. Not all at once, and not in a big way. It was more like a whisper than a shout. A quiet thought that maybe, just maybe, my brain wasn't done yet. It might have still been being built.

I remember when this idea first came to me. I was in a seminar and only half-listening to a neuroscientist talk about something called neuroplasticity. I had heard the word before, but I didn't pay much attention. It sounded like something you would only find in textbooks and research papers. But then the speaker said something that made me sit up straight. "Your brain can change at any age. It changes itself based on how you act, what you think, and how you feel. "You are not stuck." That last part hit me hard. You are not stuck.

I held on to those words for weeks. During quiet times, like when I was brushing my teeth or waiting in line at the store, they kept coming back to me. I began to think about what I would want to change if my brain could change. What patterns did I think were set in stone when they weren't? What stories had I been telling myself that weren't helping me anymore?

One of the first things I noticed was how often I went back to being anxious. It was like a reflex. When something small went wrong, like missing an email, getting a late bill, or having a fight with a friend, my mind would jump to the worst possible outcome. I didn't even know I was doing it. It happened without thinking. But now that I know more about neuroplasticity, I started to doubt that reflex. I began to watch it, softly and without judging it. I would catch myself spiraling and say, "There it is again." Not with shame, but with interest.

I started making small changes to see what happened. When I felt anxious, I would stop and take three deep breaths. I would tell myself that the brain learns from repetition, and every time I chose to stay calm instead of panicking, I was making a new neural pathway. It was strange at first, like trying to write with my left hand. But it got easier over time. There was more space between the stimulus and the response. I had a choice.

I also looked into self-talk. I didn't know how hard I was on myself until I started to pay attention. When I made a mistake, I would say things like, "You're so dumb" or "Why can't you get it right?" These words were familiar, almost comforting in how mean they were. They made me believe that I was not good enough, flawed, or deserving.

I started over with the script. Not with empty promises, but with kindness. I would say, "It's okay," when I made a mistake. You're learning. Or, "Everyone makes mistakes." "You are still growing." At first, it seemed fake. My mind fought back. But I kept going. I knew that doing it over and over was important. And over time, the new language started to stick. I began to believe it. I began to feel it.

One of the most powerful things that happened to me on this trip was working with a client who had been through a lot of trauma. She thought she was broken and couldn't be fixed. Her mind was dark, and her heart was heavy. But she was also very brave. She came every week and was willing to work. We talked about how the brain changes and heals, which is called neuroplasticity. At first, she wasn't sure, but she was interested.

We started with small things like journaling, mindfulness, and movement. She began to see changes. She slept better. She felt better. She started to laugh again. She said, "I didn't think I could change one day." "But I'm changing." I'll always remember how she looked at me. It was like seeing someone come back to themselves. She used art to help herself, and after months of therapy, she started writing poems to go with her art. Now she is the author of her own work.

That's what makes neuroplasticity so amazing. It's not only science; it's also hope. It's the idea that your brain can heal, no matter where you've been or what you've been through. Of getting bigger. Of changing into something else.

I've seen it happen to me too. I used to have trouble putting things off. I would put off tasks until the last minute, then panic and rush through them. I couldn't get out of that cycle. But after I learned how habits form in the brain, I looked at it differently. I started small by setting a timer for ten minutes and working on a task without any stress. Even if I only made a little progress, I gave myself a reward afterward. My brain started to link work with happiness instead of fear over time. The habit changed. The cycle was broken.

I also learned how important the environment is. The brain reacts to signals, and changing those signals can help it rewire itself. I made my workspace more welcoming by moving things around. I put in plants, soft lighting, and music that made me feel better. I made up rituals for myself, like lighting a candle before I wrote and stretching before meetings. These little changes told my brain that it was time to pay attention and be there. And they did work.

Sleep was also very important. I used to give up sleep to get more done, thinking I could push through tiredness. But sleep is when the brain puts memories together, gets rid of toxins, and heals itself. I started making it a priority by setting a bedtime, turning off screens, and making a calming routine. I felt like my mind was clearer. My feelings are more in balance. I was stronger.

Food was important too. I began to notice how food changed my mood and energy. I drank more water, ate more whole foods, and cut back on sugar. It wasn't about losing weight; it was about getting enough food. I noticed that when I took care of my body, my brain did too.

Moving around became a daily habit. Not hard workouts, but gentle, fun movement. Walking, dancing, and stretching. I felt more in touch with myself every time I moved. More stable. More alive. Movement is good for the brain because it makes you feel better, helps you think better, and lowers stress. It's one of the easiest things you can do to help neuroplasticity.

I also let my creative side show. I started painting, writing poetry, and playing music again. These activities woke up parts of my brain that had been sleeping. They made me remember that I wasn't just a thinker; I was also a maker. Being creative can really make a difference. It encourages play, discovery, and new ways of looking at things.

Relationships were also a factor. I was around people who made me feel good and who believed in growth. I had conversations that made me think more deeply and pushed me to think outside the box. Connection changes the way the brain works. It builds trust, empathy, and strength. I learned how to ask for what I needed, set limits, and talk to people honestly. They learned these skills; they didn't come naturally.

One of the biggest changes happened when I started to accept being uncomfortable. It's not always easy to grow. It means facing your fears, letting go of who you used to be, and going into the unknown. But every time I did, I felt my mind expand. I could feel new paths opening up. I felt like I was becoming.

I remember walking on a trail with Kathleen my wife and the children I had never been on before. It was steep, new, and a little scary. But as I walked, I felt more sure of myself. More able. More alive. That hike became a symbol of my trip. Neuroplasticity is not a straight line; it is a winding path. Sometimes going up. Sometimes rough. But always going somewhere important.

I now think of the brain as a garden. It needs food, water, sunlight, and care. It needs to be cut back, which means getting rid of things that aren't useful anymore. It needs to be planted with new ideas, habits, and beliefs. And most importantly, it needs time. It takes time to change. But it's always possible.

Your brain is not your enemy. It's on your side. It is listening. It's learning. It needs you to show it what to do. You don't have to make all the changes at once. Begin with small things. A single breath. One idea. One option. Every one is important. Every one rewires.

You are not what you have done in the past. Your patterns do not define you. You are a chance. You are growing. You build your own mind.

Your brain is beautiful, strong, and always changing, and it's ready to be rewired.

When I first learned the difference between neuroplasticity and neurogenesis, it was like finding two hidden doors in the same hallway. One led to rewiring, which means changing the way connections work, changing old habits, and making new ones. The other led to regeneration, which is the birth of completely new neurons and new starts. Both were amazing. Both had hope. And both were going on inside me, even though I didn't know it.

I remember reading that the hippocampus, which is in charge of memory and learning, is where neurogenesis happens the most. That hit me hard. I used to think that memory was something that stayed the same, like a filing cabinet that you either kept in order or let fall into disarray. But the thought that new neurons could be born there and that my brain was still making new structures for learning and remembering was very moving.

It made me think of a patient I had at the hospital who started to have trouble remembering things when he was in his late seventies. I used to sit with him and watch him try to remember names, places, and stories. He would get mad sometimes. He would laugh sometimes. But what I noticed most was that he seemed sharper when he was doing something he liked, like telling a story, listening to music, or walking in the garden. More present. More alive.

That's when I started to get that neurogenesis isn't just a biological thing. It's about getting involved. It's about getting things going. It's about giving the brain reasons to get bigger. And it's not just for young people. Anyone of any age can have it if they are willing to take care of it.

I began doing things in a new way. I started to learn a new language. It was slow and not perfect, but it made me happy. I played games with words. I read books that aren't usually in my genre. I started gardening, which meant I had to remember the names of plants, the types of soil, and the seasons. Every new challenge felt like a present for my brain. A way of saying, "You're still growing." You can still do it.

And the science agreed, that physical activity, especially aerobic exercise, helps neurogenesis. I walked more, then. I did a dance in my kitchen. I rode my bike along winding paths. Not to lose weight. Not to count steps. But to give my brain food. To get new neurons to join the fun.

Sleep also became holy. I used to think of it as an afterthought, something I did when I had time. But now I thought of it as an important part of brain health. During deep sleep, the brain gets rid of waste, strengthens memories, and helps both neuroplasticity and neurogenesis.

I made a bedtime routine that included herbal tea, soft music, and no screens. I started to have more vivid dreams. I felt better when I woke up. More complete.

Nutrition was also a factor. Foods high in omega-3 fatty acids, antioxidants, and flavonoids could help my brain grow. So I added leafy greens, walnuts, blueberries, and fatty fish to my meals (Gómez-Pinilla, 2008; Lamport et al., 2014; Yurko-Mauro et al., 2010). I drank more water. I ate less sugar. Not perfectly, but on purpose. I started to notice a difference, not just in my body but also in my mind.

Stress, I discovered, was a major blocker of neurogenesis. Chronic stress floods the brain with cortisol, which can inhibit the birth of new neurons. That was a wake-up call. I had spent years living in a state of low-grade stress — always rushing, always worrying, always bracing for the next thing. I knew I had to change.

I began practicing mindfulness and meditation. Not as a trend, but as a lifeline. I sat quietly each morning, focusing on my breath. I noticed my thoughts without clinging to them. I allowed myself to be still, spend time praying and reading the Word of God. At first, it was hard. My mind resisted. But over time, I found peace in the practice. I felt more spacious. More grounded. More able to respond instead of reacting.

I also began to reframe my relationship with failure. For years, I had seen mistakes as proof of inadequacy. But now I understood that every error was an opportunity for growth — a chance for my brain to adapt, to learn, to rewire. I started celebrating small failures. I'd say, "Look at that — a new pathway forming." It made me braver. More willing to try. More willing to change.

One of the most beautiful things I learned was that social connection supports both neuroplasticity and neurogenesis. Meaningful relationships, deep conversations, shared laughter — these experiences light up the brain. They foster resilience. They promote growth. I began prioritizing connection. I called old friends. I made time for family dinners. I joined the gym. Each interaction felt like nourishment.

That's the thing about neuroplasticity and neurogenesis — they're not just scientific concepts. They're invitations. Invitations to live more fully. To engage more deeply. To believe in our capacity for change.

I've seen it in my clients. The woman who overcame a lifetime of self-doubt by practicing daily affirmations. The man who recovered from addiction by building new routines and relationships. The teenager who rewired his anxiety through art and movement. Each story is a testament to the brain's resilience. To its ability to heal. To its hunger for growth.

And I've seen it in myself. I'm not the same person I was five years ago. My thoughts are kinder. My habits are healthier. My reactions are softer. Not because I forced change, but because I invited it. Because I trusted my brain to meet me halfway.

Your brain is not fixed. It is fluid. It is responsive. It is waiting for you.

Start small. Learn something new. Move your body. Rest deeply. Eat with intention. Connect with others. Be kind to yourself. Each choice is a signal. Each moment is a seed. And over time, those seeds become pathways. Those pathways become patterns. Those patterns become you.

BREAKING MENTAL HABITS

THE SCIENCE OF COGNITIVE RESET

For years, I lived with the quiet assumption that my thoughts were automatic and unchangeable. That the way I reacted to stress, the way I spoke to myself, the way I interpreted the world — all of it was just "how I was wired." I didn't realize that many of those patterns weren't permanent. They were practiced. Rehearsed. Reinforced over time. And just as they were built, they could be broken.

The science of cognitive reset — the process of interrupting and reshaping mental habits — has shown us that the brain is far more adaptable than we once believed. Through neuroplasticity, we now understand that the brain can form new pathways, weaken old ones, and essentially "reset" how we think, feel, and respond (Doidge, 2007). But long before neuroscience gave us language for this, Scripture was already pointing us toward renewal.

Romans 12:2 isn't just poetic — it's practical. Paul is describing a cognitive reset. A deliberate turning away from old patterns and a movement toward new ones. He's inviting us to break mental habits that keep us stuck and to embrace the Spirit-led transformation that rewires us from the inside out.

I've experienced this firsthand. One of the most persistent mental habits I carried was self-criticism. I had a voice in my head that was quick to judge, quick to shame, quick to remind me of every shortcoming. It wasn't loud, but it was constant. And for a long time, I thought it was just part of being self-aware. But over time, I realized it was more than that — it was a habit. A reflex. A mental groove I had worn deep through repetition.

Breaking that habit didn't happen overnight. It started with noticing. With catching the voice in action. With asking, "Is this true? Is this kind? Is this how God speaks to me?" That last question was the most powerful. Because when I compared my inner voice to the voice of God in Scripture, I saw a stark difference. God's voice convicts, yes — but it also comforts. It corrects, but it never condemns. It speaks truth, but always in love.

Isaiah 30:21 says, "***Whether you turn to the right or to the left, your ears will hear a voice behind you, saying, 'This is the way; walk in it.'***" That's the voice I began to listen for. And slowly, as I replaced the harsh self-talk with Scripture, prayer, and grace-filled reflection, my mental habits began to shift.

Cognitive behavioural therapy teaches that our thoughts shape our feelings, which shape our behaviours (Beck, 2011). When we change our thoughts, we change our lives. But Scripture has been saying this all along.

Proverbs 4:23 says, *"Above all else, guard your heart, for everything you do flows from it."* The heart, in biblical language, often refers to the inner life — the seat of thought, emotion, and will. Guarding it means being intentional about what we dwell on, what we rehearse, what we believe.

Breaking mental habits also requires replacing them. Jesus speaks to this in Luke 11:24–26, where He describes a person freed from an impure spirit who doesn't fill the empty space with anything new — and ends up worse off than before. The principle is clear: when we remove something harmful, we must replace it with something holy. When we break a mental habit, we must build a new one.

For me, that meant memorizing Scripture. Speaking truth aloud. Practicing gratitude. It meant catching myself in moments of anxiety and choosing to breathe, to pray, to remember God's promises. It meant rewiring my brain with the Word of God — not just reading it, but letting it reshape me.

Philippians 4:8 became a cornerstone: *"Whatever is true, whatever is noble, whatever is right, whatever is pure... think about such things."* That verse isn't just a call to positivity — it's a cognitive reset. It's a blueprint for mental renewal. It's a way of training the mind to dwell on what is life-giving.

I've also learned that breaking mental habits is not a solo journey. We need community. We need people who remind us of truth when we forget. Hebrews 10:24–25 says, *"Let us consider how we may spur one another on toward love and good deeds... encouraging one another."* Encouragement is a powerful disruptor of negative mental loops. A kind word, a gentle reminder, a shared prayer — these are the tools God uses through others to help us reset.

There's also a spiritual dimension to cognitive reset that science can't fully explain. The Holy Spirit doesn't just inform us — He transforms us. 2 Corinthians 3:18 says, *"We all... are being transformed into His image with ever-increasing glory, which comes from the Lord, who is the Spirit.*" That transformation includes our minds. Our thoughts. Our mental habits. The Spirit renews us from the inside out, often in ways we don't even realize until we look back and see how far we've come.

Breaking mental habits also involves repentance — not just turning from sin, but turning from falsehood. From fear. From shame. Repentance is a reset. It's a reorientation. It's a return to truth. Acts 3:19 says, "*Repent... so that times of refreshing may come from the Lord.*" That refreshing includes mental clarity, emotional healing, spiritual renewal.

I've found that writing helps. Writing down my thoughts, naming the lies, replacing them with truth. It's a way of externalizing the internal. Of making the invisible visible. Of partnering with God in the renewal of my mind.

I used to think habits were just behaviours—things we did repeatedly, like brushing our teeth or checking our phones. But over time, I came to understand that habits live deeper than that. They're not just actions. They're patterns of thought. Emotional reflexes. Mental grooves worn into the brain through years of repetition. And some of them, I realized, were keeping me stuck.

There was a period in my life when I felt like I was living on autopilot. I'd wake up, scroll through my phone before even getting out of bed, rush through my morning, and spend the day reacting to everything—emails, texts, interruptions, expectations. I wasn't choosing my responses. I was just repeating them. And by the end of the day, I'd collapse into bed, exhausted but wired, wondering why I felt so disconnected from myself.

It wasn't until I started studying the science of cognitive reset that I began to understand what was happening. My brain had built a network of habits—not just physical ones, but mental ones. I had trained myself to worry, to overthink, to anticipate the worst. I had built highways of thought that my brain travelled automatically, even when those roads led nowhere good.

The science behind this is both fascinating and hopeful. Our brains are made up of billions of neurons, connected by synapses that strengthen with use. When we repeat a thought or behaviour, those connections become more efficient. It's like carving a path through a forest—the more you walk it, the clearer it becomes. This is how habits form. But here's the beautiful part: those paths can be changed. New ones can be carved. Old ones can fade. That's the essence of cognitive reset.

I remember the first time I tried to break a mental habit. It was the habit of self-criticism. Every time I made a mistake, my inner voice would pounce: "You always mess things up." "Why can't you get it right?" "You're not good enough." I didn't even notice it at first. It was just background noise. But once I became aware of it, I was shocked by how often it showed up.

So I began to interrupt it. Gently. When I caught myself thinking something harsh, I'd pause and say, "That's not true." Or, "You're learning." Or sometimes just, "Be kind." At first, it felt awkward. Forced. But I kept at it. I knew that repetition was key. And slowly, the old voice began to quiet. A new one began to emerge—one that was softer, more compassionate, more truthful.

This process wasn't linear. There were days I slipped back into old patterns. Days I forgot to pause. But I learned that breaking mental habits isn't about perfection. It's about awareness. About choosing again and again to take a different path.

One of the most powerful tools I discovered was mindfulness and mediation in God's Word. Not the trendy kind, but the simple practice of noticing. I'd sit quietly each morning, focusing on my breath. When thoughts came, I'd observe them without judgment. I began to see how often my mind wandered into worry, comparison, or planning. And instead of following those thoughts, I learned to let them pass. To return to the present.

This practice rewired my brain. It gave me space between stimulus and response. It helped me catch myself before I spiraled. And over time, it changed the way I thought—not just during meditation, but throughout the day.

I also began to understand the role of triggers. Mental habits don't exist in isolation. They're often tied to specific cues—a place, a person, a time of day. For me, checking my phone first thing in the morning was a trigger for anxiety. I'd see emails, news, social media, and immediately feel overwhelmed. So I changed the cue. I left my phone in another room. I started my day with journaling instead. That small shift made a big difference. It set a new tone. It carved a new path.

Another habit I worked on was catastrophizing—jumping to worst-case scenarios. If someone didn't reply to a message, I'd assume they were upset. If I felt a headache, I'd worry it was something serious. These thoughts felt real, urgent, convincing. But they were just habits. My brain had learned to protect me by anticipating danger. It meant well. But it was exhausting.

So I practiced reframing. When a fearful thought arose, I'd ask, "Is this true?" "Is there another explanation?" "What would I tell a friend in this situation?" These questions helped me step outside the habit. They gave me perspective. And with time, my brain learned a new way to respond—one rooted in calm, not fear.

I also leaned into movement. Physical habits and mental habits are deeply connected. When I felt stuck in my thoughts, I'd go for a walk. Stretch. Dance. Move my body in any way that felt good. This wasn't about fitness. It was about flow. About reminding my brain that change is possible. That energy can shift. That I am not my thoughts—I am the one who observes them.

One of the most surprising discoveries was how much language matters. The words we use shape our thoughts. I used to say, "I'm terrible at this," or "I always mess up." Now I say, "I'm learning," or "This is new for me." These shifts may seem small, but they're powerful. They send different signals to the brain. They reinforce different pathways. They build new habits.

I've seen this transformation in others, too. A client who used to say, "I'm just an anxious person," began to say, "I'm learning to feel safe." Another who said, "I can't change," began to say, "I'm practicing something new." These changes weren't just semantic. They were cognitive resets. They were new scripts for the brain to follow.

Breaking mental habits is not about force. It's about compassion. About curiosity. About gently guiding the brain toward new patterns. It takes time. It takes patience. But it's possible. And it's worth it.

I still have habits I'm working on. I still catch myself falling into old grooves. But now I know I have the tools. I know I have the awareness. I know I can choose a different path.

You are not your habits. You are the one who shapes them. You are the one who chooses. You are the one who grows.

There's something quietly powerful about realizing that your thoughts are not facts. That the mental habits you've carried for years — the ones that whisper "you're not good enough," or "this will never work," or "you always mess things up" — are not truths etched into your identity. They're patterns. Learned responses. Neural loops that can be interrupted, softened, and eventually replaced.

I remember sitting with a client who had spent most of her adult life believing she was a burden. It wasn't something she said out loud often, but it lived in her choices — in the way she apologized for speaking, in the way she hesitated to ask for help, in the way she shrank herself in relationships. One day, I asked her where that belief came from. She paused, then said, "I think I just got used to feeling that way." That sentence stayed with me. I got used to feeling that way.

That's the essence of a mental habit. It's not always dramatic. It's often subtle, familiar, and deeply ingrained. It's the emotional posture we assume without realizing. The lens through which we interpret the world. And the science tells us that these habits are not fixed. They're flexible. They're built on neural pathways that can be rewired through awareness, repetition, and intentional change.

Cognitive reset begins with noticing. Noticing the thought that always shows up when you make a mistake. Noticing the story you tell yourself when someone doesn't text back. Noticing the way your mind jumps to judgment, or fear, or shame. This noticing is not passive — it's active, compassionate, and curious. It's the moment you step outside the habit and say, "Ah, there you are."

The brain is a prediction machine. It likes efficiency. It builds shortcuts based on past experience. If you've spent years responding to stress with panic, your brain will default to that response. If you've spent years interpreting silence as rejection, your brain will fill in that blank with fear. But here's the miracle: every time you choose a different response, you weaken the old pathway and strengthen a new one. You're not just thinking differently — you're physically changing your brain.

I've seen this in my own life. I used to have a habit of over-preparing. For meetings, for conversations, even for casual outings. I'd rehearse what I was going to say, anticipate every possible outcome, and try to control the narrative. It came from a place of anxiety — a fear of being caught off guard, of not being enough. But it was exhausting. And it kept me from being present.

So I started practicing trust. I'd walk into a meeting with just a few notes. I'd let conversations unfold naturally. I'd remind myself, "You can handle whatever comes." At first, it felt reckless. My brain protested. But over time, the anxiety softened. The habit loosened. And

I discovered something beautiful: I was more authentic. More connected. More alive.

Breaking mental habits also involves understanding the emotional payoff. Every habit, even the painful ones, serves a purpose. Self-criticism might give us a sense of control. Worry might make us feel prepared. Avoidance might protect us from discomfort. But when we name the payoff, we can begin to question it. Is this really helping me? Is there a gentler way?

I worked with a man who had a habit of withdrawing whenever he felt hurt. He'd shut down, go silent, and retreat into himself. It was his way of protecting his vulnerability. But it also created distance in his relationships. When he began to notice the pattern, he asked himself, "What am I afraid of?" The answer was rejection. So we practiced a new habit — staying present, expressing his feelings, asking for reassurance. It was hard. But it changed everything.

The science supports this. When we engage in new behaviours, especially ones that challenge old patterns, we activate neuroplasticity — the brain's ability to reorganize itself. We create new synaptic connections. We shift from automatic to intentional. And with repetition, the new habit becomes the default.

But repetition alone isn't enough. Emotion matters. The brain learns best when the experience is emotionally charged. That's why breakthroughs often happen during moments of vulnerability, connection, or insight. When you feel something deeply — whether it's joy, sadness, or relief — your brain pays attention. It remembers. It rewires.

I often encourage clients to pair new habits with emotional anchors. If you're practicing self-compassion, do it while looking at a photo of someone you love. If you're trying to break a habit of avoidance, take a deep breath and recall a time you felt brave. These anchors create resonance. They make the new habit stick.

Our surroundings cue our behaviours. If your phone is the first thing you see in the morning, it becomes a trigger for distraction. If your workspace is cluttered, it might reinforce overwhelm. Changing your environment can support cognitive reset. Put your journal by your bed. Leave your phone in another room. Create spaces that invite presence.

I remember a woman who had a habit of people-pleasing. She said yes to everything, even when it drained her. She feared conflict, rejection, and being seen as selfish. But she was tired. So we practiced saying no. At first, she whispered it. Then she said it with a shaky voice. Eventually, she said it with confidence. And each time, her brain rewired. She began to feel her own worth. She began to trust her own voice.

That's the heart of cognitive reset. It's not about erasing who you've been. It's about reclaiming who you are. It's about choosing presence over pattern. Intention over impulse. Truth over habit.

You are not your automatic thoughts. You are the awareness behind them. You are the one who chooses. You are the one who grows.

I've also learned to celebrate progress. Breaking mental habits is slow work. It's daily work. And every time I catch a thought, choose a new one, and act on it — that's victory. That's growth. That's transformation.

So if you're stuck in a mental loop — of anxiety, shame, fear, criticism — I want you to know: you're not alone. And you're not stuck forever. Your brain can reset. Your mind can renew. Your thoughts can change.

Start with Scripture. Start with prayer. Start with noticing. And trust that the God who made your mind also made a way for it to heal.

You are not your patterns. You are not your past. You are a new creation.

And your mind — beloved, capable, Spirit-filled — is ready to be renewed.

ADJUST YOUR THINKING

AN INVITATION TO TRANSFORMATION

Adjust your thinking isn't just a suggestion; it's an invitation to change. Both science and the Bible softly tell you, "*You don't have to stay stuck.*" You can change—not just your habits or your situation, but also how your mind works. Neuroplasticity is a miracle, and the Bible talks about the promise of renewal all the time. Neuroscience and Scripture are not in conflict; they actually work together in a way that feels like a divine duet, each one echoing the truth that our thoughts shape our lives.

Let's start with the idea that your brain can change. For hundreds of years, people thought that your brain was set in stone once you became an adult. But modern neuroscience has shown us something much more hopeful.

Your brain is more like clay—it can change, respond, and be molded. Neuroplasticity is the name for this. It means that your thoughts can actually change the structure of your brain over time. Isn't that amazing? The pathways and grooves in your mind are not set in stone. They can be healed, rerouted, and made new.

A lot of what Dr. Caroline Leaf, a cognitive neuroscientist and devout Christian, has written is about this. She calls it "*self-directed neuroplasticity*," which means that you can change your brain by changing the way you think. She writes, "*When you understand the power of your thought life… you truly begin to get a glimpse of how important it is to take responsibility for what you are thinking*" (Leaf, C., 2021).

This aligns beautifully with what the Apostle Paul wrote in Romans 12:2, a key scripture we have used several times in this book, "***Do not conform to the pattern of this world, but be transformed by the renewing of your mind.***" Paul didn't have access to brain scans or scientific journals, but he understood something profound: transformation begins in the mind.

Take a moment to think about that. The idea of "*renewing your mind*" isn't just a poetic phrase; it's a fact about how your brain works. Your brain starts to make new connections when you choose to think about love, hope, and truth. When you stop being afraid, angry, or ashamed, those old paths start to fade away. It's like walking through a forest and picking a new path—the more you walk it, the easier it gets to see. The old path that no one uses anymore becomes overgrown and disappears. That's what happens in your brain when you change the way you think.

But let's be real. Adjust your thinking isn't always easy. Our thoughts can feel like wild horses running in all directions. They can feel like heavy chains pulling us down. And sometimes, they feel like old friends, even when they're hurting us. That's why the Bible doesn't just tell us to change our minds; it also tells us how to do it. Paul says in 2 Corinthians 10:5, "*We take captive every thought to make it obedient to Christ*." This is active language—it's not passive. It's not waiting for your mind to settle down. It's stepping in and saying, "*No, this thought doesn't belong here,*" in a calm but firm way.

When you consciously adjust your thinking, you activate parts of your brain that help you make decisions and control your emotions. You're not just thinking differently; you're also using your brain in a way that helps it heal and grow. Reading the Bible, praying, and meditating have all been shown to strengthen these parts of the brain. It seems like God made your brain to respond to what He says.

Let's take a moment to think about Jesus. He was a master at changing how He thought. He chose peace over fear. He chose to be still when things were chaotic. He chose truth when He was tempted by lies. Satan tried to twist Scripture in the wilderness, but Jesus answered clearly and with conviction. He didn't let the enemy change how He thought; He changed how He thought with the Word of God. That's what we want to do—not only to fight off negative thoughts but also to replace them with better ones.

This is where grace comes in. Adjust your thinking isn't about being perfect; it's about direction. It's about making the choice to align your thoughts with the truth in every moment. And when you fail, which you will, grace will be there to catch you. The brain doesn't change in a day—it takes time, practice, and kindness. So be gentle with yourself. Celebrate little wins. It's progress when you notice a bad thought and choose a better one. That's a change.

David understood this. He wrote in Psalm 139, "*Search me, God, and know my heart; test me and know my anxious thoughts*." He didn't try to hide his thoughts from God—he let Him in. Inviting God into your mind is the first step in changing how you think. Not just in your prayers, but in your daily thoughts—your fears, your hopes, and your doubts. He's not indifferent to them; He wants to walk with you through them.

Keep this in mind, your thoughts are like seeds. You will reap what you plant. If you plant fear, you will grow anxiety. If you plant bitterness, you'll harvest anger. But if you plant truth, you will grow peace. If you plant love, you will grow joy. This is what neuroscience says too: the more you think about something, the stronger it becomes. So pick your seeds carefully. Water them with the Word of God. Feed them with prayer. And see what happens.

Adjust your thinking isn't something you do once; it's something you do every day as part of a sacred cycle of renewal. It's waking up each day and deciding which thoughts to keep, which beliefs to nurture, and which lies to let go of. The Bible calls this "*renewing your mind*," and neuroscience calls it "*rewiring your brain*." Both say the same thing: your thoughts aren't just passing ideas—they shape your reality.

There are about 86 billion neurons in the human brain, and each one can make thousands of connections. Synapses are the connections where thoughts live. The more you think about something, the stronger those synapses become. It's like cutting a groove into a piece of wood—the deeper the groove, the easier it is for your mind to go down that path. Over time, this is why habits of thought, good or bad, become automatic (Doidge, 2007).

The good news is that those grooves don't last forever. Neuroplasticity allows your brain to make new connections and break old ones. This means you can start to change even if you've been thinking negatively for a long time. You can choose new thoughts, and if you think them over and over again with purpose, they will become your new default. It's not magic—it's biology. And it's also grace.

Romans 12:2 advised us to renew our minds. The Greek word for "renewing" here is *anakainosis*, which means a complete renovation—not just a touch-up on the surface, but a deep change at the core.

Paul wants us to do more than just think positively; he wants us to think truthfully—to make our thoughts match those of Christ. And when we do, things change.

This change is not only spiritual; it is also physical. Research indicates that activities such as prayer and meditation can alter the brain's structure. Dr. Andrew Newberg, a neuroscientist who studies how religious practices affect the brain, found that prayer and meditation make the prefrontal cortex more active. This is the part of the brain that controls focus, decision-making, and empathy (Newberg & Waldman, 2009). When you do spiritual things, you're not just getting closer to God—you're also making your brain stronger.

This is why the Bible is so powerful. When you meditate on God's Word, you're not just reading it; you're changing how your brain works. "***But his delight is in the law of the Lord, and on his law he meditates day and night,***" says Psalm 1:2–3. He is like a tree planted by streams of water. Meditation isn't something you do passively; it's something you do actively. It's deciding to think about the truth until it becomes a part of you. When it does, you become like that tree—strong, rooted, and unshakable.

Let's talk about the kinds of thoughts that need to be changed. Often, they're not the loud ones. They're the quiet thoughts that run through our minds all the time: "***I'll never change,*" "*I'm not enough,*" "*God doesn't care.***" They might *feel* true, but they're not—and the longer they stay, the more damage they do. That's why Paul tells us in 2 Corinthians 10:5 to "***take every thought captive.***" Not just the obvious ones, but also the subtle ones—the ones that slip in unnoticed.

To take a thought captive means to look at it—to shine the light of truth on it. To ask, "*Is this thought helping or hurting me? Is it aligned with God's Word or with fear?*" This is where neuroscience and the Bible meet again. Cognitive Behavioral Therapy (CBT), a well-known approach in mental health, teaches people to identify and challenge distorted thoughts. It's remarkably similar to what Paul says: you don't just accept every thought at face value—you question it. You replace lies with truth.

Dr. Jeffrey Schwartz, a psychiatrist and researcher, developed a method called the "*Four Steps*" to help people change the way their brains work. The steps are: *Relabel, Reattribute, Refocus, and Revalue.* When a bad thought comes to mind, you change the label on it ("This is a lie"), change the reason for it ("This is coming from a faulty brain pattern"), focus on something good or useful, and change its value ("This doesn't deserve my attention") (Schwartz & Begley, 2002). It's a good way to follow what the Bible says about "*renewing your mind.*"

But we shouldn't forget about the heart. Changing the way you think isn't just a mental exercise; it's a spiritual surrender. It means saying, "*God, I want to see myself the way You see me. I want to think thoughts that reflect Your love, Your truth, and Your grace.*" It's an invitation for the Holy Spirit to be your thought partner and inner counselor. He is the Spirit of Truth, and He loves to help you think freely.

Awareness is the first step to freedom. You can't change what you don't see. So pay attention. Listen to what you say to yourself. What do you tell yourself when you wake up? When you make a mistake? When you're alone? Those thoughts matter. They shape how you feel, what you do, and who you become. "**Guard your heart above all else, for everything you do flows from it,**" says Proverbs 4:23. In Hebrew, the word for "*heart*" often includes the mind. Take care of your thoughts, because they are the source of your life.

And don't feel bad about yourself when you catch a thought that doesn't belong. Don't spiral. Just stop. Take a breath. Re-route. That's the beauty of grace: it meets you where you are. It doesn't wait for things to be perfect—it walks with you through the steps. Philippians 4:8 gives us a beautiful way to sort through our thoughts: "*Whatever is true, whatever is noble, whatever is right, whatever is pure, whatever is lovely, whatever is admirable—if anything is excellent or praiseworthy—think about such things*." This isn't just poetry; it's practical. It's a mental health guide.

Positive thinking has been associated with reduced stress, improved cardiovascular health, and enhanced resilience (Fredrickson, 2001). It's not about ignoring pain; it's about choosing hope. It's about having faith that light can break through even in the darkest times. That's what the Bible says. Neuroscience confirms it. What you think matters. Your thoughts change your mind, your spirit, and your life.

When you start to change the way you think, something amazing happens—you begin to see yourself differently. Not through your past, your failures, or your fears, but through the lens of grace. You start to see yourself the way God sees you: loved, chosen, and capable of change. And that change, though it may begin small, starts to influence every part of your life. It alters your self-talk, your reactions to others, and your approach to challenges. It's not just a change in how you think; it's a change in who you are.

Neuroscience says that repeated patterns of thought shape who we become. The more you say, "*I'm not good enough*," the more your brain believes it. But the opposite is also true. When you start to say, "*I am loved,*" or "*I am being renewed,*" your brain begins to build that reality. It's not just wishful thinking—it's biology. Your brain is paying attention to you. So, speak life.

This is why affirmations are so powerful when they're based on truth. They are more than motivational slogans; they are tools for transformation. When you say, "*I can do all things through Christ who strengthens me*" (Philippians 4:13), you're not just quoting the Bible; you're strengthening a neural pathway of hope.

When you say, "*I am fearfully and wonderfully made*" (Psalm 139:14), you're not just reciting a verse; you're reshaping how you see yourself. These words matter. They help your brain heal by building new bridges.

Adjust your thinking is really about healing. It's not just about being more productive or happy; it's about becoming whole. We all have wounds in our minds—memories, beliefs, and voices from the past that tell lies that sound true: "*You'll always be this way.*" "*You're too broken to change.*" "*God has forgotten you.*" These thoughts are not only painful but also paralyzing. They keep us trapped in cycles of fear and shame.

But the Bible tells a different story. Isaiah 43:18–19 says, "*Forget the former things; do not dwell on the past. See, I am doing a new thing!*" God is not limited by your past. Your patterns don't hold Him back. He is always doing something new—and that newness starts in your mind. When you choose to let go of old thoughts and embrace new ones, you are participating in the new thing God is doing.

That participation is real, and it takes effort. Neuroscience indicates that deliberate thought—what researchers call *"focused attention"*—activates the brain's executive functions. These are the areas responsible for planning, decision-making, and self-control. When you focus on the truth, you're not just changing your thoughts—you're strengthening your ability to live differently. It's a cycle: thinking correctly leads to living correctly, which reinforces correct thinking.

Paul understood this when he told the Colossians, "*Set your minds on things above, not on earthly things*" (Colossians 3:2). The word "*set*" implies intention and effort. It's like setting a compass—you don't just drift toward truth; you align yourself with it. When you wander, you return to it. And in that return, you find grace.

Grace is the foundation of all mental transformation. Without it, changing the way you think becomes exhausting—an endless effort to be better, think better, do better. But with grace, it becomes a journey, a process, a relationship with God. You're not walking it alone. The Holy Spirit is your guide, your comforter, and your counselor. He doesn't just reveal truth; He walks with you into it.

In John 14:26, Jesus said, "***But the Advocate, the Holy Spirit... will teach you all things and will remind you of everything I have said to you.***" This includes the truth about who you are. When fear creeps in, the Spirit brings you back to peace. When your mind is filled with shame, He whispers grace. When you forget your worth, He reminds you of your value. This isn't abstract—it's personal. It's intimate. It's real.

So don't give up. Adjust your thinking isn't a destination; it's a daily journey. Some days will feel easy; others will feel like a fight. But every step counts. Every thought matters. Every time you fall and start again, it's another seed planted. Over time, those seeds will grow into a garden of peace, joy, and truth.

THE CHALLENGE

CHANGING HABITS DUE TO COMPETITIVE PLASTICITY

For years, I thought changing a habit was simply a matter of motivation. If I wanted it badly enough, I'd change. I'd set goals, make plans, and start strong. But inevitably, I'd slip. I'd fall back into old patterns. And I'd wonder, "Why is this so hard?" It wasn't until I learned about competitive plasticity that I began to understand the deeper challenge.

Competitive plasticity is the principle that neural pathways in the brain compete for dominance. The more a pathway is used — whether it's a behaviour, a thought pattern, or a reaction — the stronger it becomes. When we try to build a new habit, we're not just creating something new. We're competing with something old, something familiar, something deeply ingrained (Doidge, 2007). This concept helped me make sense of my own struggles. I wasn't failing. I was rewiring.

I remember trying to break the habit of negative self-talk. I'd catch myself saying things like, "You're not good enough," or "You always mess this up." I knew those thoughts weren't true. I knew they were hurting me. But they were automatic. They had been rehearsed for years. And every time I tried to replace them with truth — "You're growing," "You're loved," "You're doing your best" — it felt awkward. Forced. Like I was speaking a language I hadn't yet learned.

That's competitive plasticity in action. The old pathways were strong. The new ones were weak. And the brain, being efficient, always defaults to what's familiar. As Merzenich (2013) explains, the brain is constantly reshaping itself based on use. The circuits we activate most often become dominant, while unused ones fade. So when we try to change, we're asking our brain to shift its allegiance — and that takes time.

But here's what I've learned: change is possible. It's just slower than we expect. It's not about flipping a switch. It's about rewiring a system. And that takes repetition, patience, and grace.

Romans 12:2 speaks directly to this process: "***Do not conform to the pattern of this world, but be transformed by the renewing of your mind.***" Paul isn't describing a one-time event. He's describing a daily practice. A slow, steady rewiring. The Greek word for "renewing" (ἀνακαίνωσις) implies ongoing renovation — a continual process of change.

I started with small verses. Truths I could carry with me. "***I am fearfully and wonderfully made***" (Psalm 139:14). "***There is no condemnation for those who are in Christ Jesus***" (Romans 8:1). "***The Lord is my shepherd; I lack nothing***" (Psalm 23:1). I'd write them on sticky notes. Say them out loud. Whisper them in moments of doubt. And slowly, those new pathways began to form.

But it wasn't just about repetition. It was about relationship. I wasn't just trying to change my brain — I was inviting God into the process. I'd pray, "Lord, help me think differently. Help me see myself the way You see me. Help me choose truth over fear." And He did. Not instantly. Not dramatically. But faithfully.

I've also learned that competitive plasticity doesn't just apply to thoughts — it applies to behaviours. I used to have a habit of checking my phone first thing in the morning. Before I prayed. Before I breathed. Before I even got out of bed. It was automatic. And every time I tried to change it — to start my day with silence, or Scripture, or gratitude — I'd feel the pull. The itch. The reflex.

I made a small change. I moved my Bible to my nightstand and my phone across the room. I gave the new habit a fighting chance. And over time, the morning reflex shifted. Not perfectly. Not every day. But enough to feel the difference.

That's the key with competitive plasticity: we have to make space for the new. We have to protect it. Prioritize it. Practice it. And we have to be patient when it feels unnatural.

I remember talking to a friend who was trying to build a habit of journaling. He'd start strong, then forget for days. He felt discouraged. But when we talked about competitive plasticity, something clicked. He realized he wasn't failing — he was competing. The old habit of rushing through his mornings was strong. The new habit of reflection was still growing. And that awareness gave him grace. It helped him keep going.

Grace is essential in this process. Because change is hard. Not because we're weak, but because our brains are wired for efficiency. They prefer the known. The practiced. The familiar. And when we try to change, we're asking our brain to do something inefficient. Something uncomfortable. Something new.

But Scripture reminds us that we're not doing it alone. Philippians 1:6 says, *"He who began a good work in you will carry it on to completion."* That includes our habits. Our thoughts. Our neural pathways. God is in the rewiring. He's in the repetition. He's in the slow, sacred work of transformation.

I've also learned that competitive plasticity can work in our favour. Once a new habit gains strength, it begins to crowd out the old. The more I practice gratitude, the less room there is for complaint. The more I speak truth, the quieter the lies become. The more I choose presence, the less I crave distraction.

It's not about perfection. It's about progress. About choosing the new path one more time than the old. About trusting that every small choice matters.

I've seen this in my spiritual life too. I used to struggle with consistency in prayer. I'd start strong, then drift. But when I began to see prayer as a habit — a neural pathway — I approached it differently. I set reminders. I created space. I practiced. And slowly, prayer became less of a task and more of a rhythm. A reflex. A joy.

Competitive plasticity also reminds me to be gentle with others. When someone is trying to change — to break a habit, to think differently, to grow — I remember how hard it is. I remember the competition in the brain. The pull of the familiar. The discomfort of the new. And I offer grace. Encouragement. Patience.

Galatians 6:2 says, *"Carry each other's burdens, and in this way you will fulfill the law of Christ."* That includes the burden of change. The burden of rewiring. The burden of competing pathways.

So if you're trying to change a habit — to think differently, live differently, love differently — I want you to know: you're not failing. You're competing. And every time you choose the new path, you're winning.

Start small. Repeat often. Invite God in. And trust that the brain He designed is capable of renewal.

You are not your old patterns. You are not your past reflexes. You are a new creation.

And your mind — resilient, responsive, Spirit-filled — is ready to grow.

DIGITAL DETOX

RECLAIMING FOCUS IN A DISTRACTED WORLD

I didn't know how distracted I had gotten until I tried to sit still. No phone. No music. No alerts. It's just me, a journal, and God. My mind was racing in a matter of minutes. I grabbed my phone without thinking. I wasn't looking for anything important; I just didn't like being still. That moment woke me up. I had gotten so used to always getting information that I had forgotten how to be in the moment. How to pay attention. How to take a break.

There is always noise around us. Everywhere you look, screens are glowing. Notifications sound like little alarms. Algorithms give us more of what we already believe. Technology has made life much easier, but it has also slowly taken away our attention, presence, and peace. We think less and scroll more. We pray less than we react. We eat more than we connect.

Digital detox is more than just a trendy way to be healthy; it's a spiritual practice. It's a conscious decision to put down your phone and other digital devices so you can get your mind back on track, strengthen your relationships, and reconnect with God. And the Bible has a lot to say about this.

"*Be still and know that I am God*," says Psalm 46:10. That verse is more than just a poem; it's a command. Be quiet. Not just in your body, but also in your mind. In an emotional way. In a spiritual way. In a culture that values hard work and doing many things at once, being still seems strange.

We can hear God's voice when we are quiet. Elijah didn't find God in the wind, the earthquake, or the fire. Instead, he found Him in the soft voice (1 Kings 19:11–12). Digital noise often drowns out that whisper.

Long before smartphones were invented, Jesus showed how to do a digital detox. He often went to quiet places to pray (Luke 5:16). He got away from people, noise, and demands. He didn't just teach people how to be alone; he did it himself. We need space to reconnect with God even more than the Son of God did.

I have noticed that something changes when I take a break from screens, even for a short time. My mind slows down. My prayers become deeper. I become more aware. I see the beauty in the world around me, like the way leaves feel, the way I breathe, and the way a stranger smiles at me. I become more aware of what's going on around me. More stable. More alive.

I have quoted this scripture many times and here it is again, "*Do not conform to the pattern of this world, but be transformed by the renewing of your mind*," says Romans 12:2. One way we resist conformity is by taking a break from technology. It's a way of saying, "I won't let someone else take over my mind." I won't let algorithms change how I think. I choose renewal." That renewal doesn't happen through more content — it happens through more connection. With God. With other people. With ourselves.

One of the biggest changes I've noticed since going digital detox is that I can be more intentional. When I don't have to respond to notifications all the time, I start to think more carefully about what I do. I ask, "What is most important today?" "Who needs me to be there?" "How can I help?" That change from reacting to thinking is very biblical. "Let your eyes look straight ahead... give careful thought to the paths for your feet," says Proverbs 4:25–27. To be that focused, you need space. It needs to be quiet. It needs to be detoxed.

Digital detox also helps us get back our Sabbath. The Sabbath isn't just a day off; it's a holy time to rest and heal. *"Remember the Sabbath day by keeping it holy,"* says Exodus 20:8. In today's world, keeping the Sabbath holy might mean turning off our devices. It could mean picking being there over getting things done. It might mean having faith that the world will keep going even if we're not online.

I now take short breaks during the week. A few hours without screens. A walk without music. A meal without scrolling. These times have become holy. Not because they're perfect, but because they mean something. They remind me that what I do doesn't define me. That I am loved, even when I am not online.

Digital detox also shows us who we look up to. I ask myself, "What am I afraid of missing?" when I feel anxious without my phone. I ask myself, "What am I trying to get away from?" when I'm bored and not scrolling. These questions reveal deeper truths. Sometimes I realize I've been looking for likes to prove my worth. I've used entertainment to numb pain. There have been times when I've stayed away from God. Detox reveals these patterns—not to make us feel bad, but to set us free.

Hebrews 12:1 says, *"Let us throw off everything that hinders… and run with perseverance the race marked out for us."* Digital distractions aren't evil in themselves, but they slowly eat away at us.

They make us go slower. They make it hard to focus. They lessen our devotion. Throwing them off doesn't mean giving up on technology; it means taking back control of it.

I now ask myself, "Am I serving this tool, or is it serving me?" That question helps me reset. It helps me make good choices. It helps me treat my attention as a gift.

Digital detox also gives us time to connect with others on a deeper level. I look people in the eye when I put my phone down. I pay more attention. I laugh more easily. I connect more deeply. James 1:19 says, *"Everyone should be quick to listen, slow to speak…"* To listen, you have to be present. And being present takes focus. Detox helps us give that attention freely.

If I had been staring at a screen, these conversations would never have happened. I've seen pain in someone's eyes. I've heard happiness in someone's voice. The Spirit has nudged me to pray, to love, and to encourage. These moments are sacred. And we often miss them when we're busy.

I didn't know how much I had lost until I tried to sit still—not just in body, but in mind. I had set aside an hour to write, something I used to love. I made tea, cleaned off my desk, opened my notebook… and then picked up my phone. I told myself it was just for a second, just to check the time. But that second turned into twenty minutes of scrolling, clicking, and responding. When I looked up, the tea was cold and the page was still blank.

That was when I realized something had to change.

It wasn't just about getting things done. It was about being present. About reclaiming the ability to be alone with myself. I had become so accustomed to distraction that silence felt uncomfortable. I had trained my brain to crave stimulation, to seek novelty, and to resist stillness. And I wasn't alone.

The world we live in is designed to steal our attention. Notifications, headlines, and endless feeds are built to capture us, keep us engaged, and make us forget what we were doing. It's not your fault—it's cultural. But it affects us. It shows up in how we feel about ourselves, how we sleep, how we relate to others, and how creative we are.

I started to notice the signs. I couldn't finish a book. I'd start a movie and check my phone halfway through. I'd walk into a room and forget why. My thoughts scattered like leaves in the wind. I was always multitasking, but never really present. And underneath it all was a quiet worry—that I was missing something, falling behind, and never quite enough.

So I made a big change. I shut it all down. Not forever. Not completely. But enough to notice the difference. I'd leave my phone in the bathroom or somewhere out of reach for a few hours. I started with a weekend. No social media. No emails. No news. I kept my phone on in case of emergency and told a few close friends what I was doing. Then I stepped into the quiet.

It was disorienting at first. I kept reaching for my phone out of habit. My fingers moved on their own. I lost my train of thought. I felt like I couldn't be alone with myself. But over time, things changed. I started to notice the sound of birds, the way light moved across the floor, the rhythm of my own breathing. I felt more grounded. More alive.

That weekend, I read, walked, and journaled. I cooked slowly. I listened to music without skipping songs. I had conversations uninterrupted by pings or vibrations. And by Sunday night, I felt something I hadn't felt in a long time: clarity.

It wasn't just about removing screens. It was about reclaiming space—mental space, emotional space, creative space. I realized my attention was a limited resource, and I had been giving it away without thought. Every scroll, every click, every notification was like withdrawing from my mental bank account. And I was running on empty.

Science backs this up. Our brains aren't built for constant stimulation. The prefrontal cortex, which handles decision-making and focus, gets overwhelmed. We stop reflecting and start reacting. Our stress rises. Over time, we lose touch with our inner compass.

Digital detox isn't about rejecting technology. It's about redefining our relationship with it. It's about using it intentionally, not automatically. We're not machines—we're humans with needs, limits, and rhythms.

After that weekend, I built new habits. I made parts of my home phone-free—like the dining table and the bedroom. I stopped checking my phone first thing in the morning. I began my day with breath, movement, and quiet. I checked email only at set times. I turned off non-essential notifications. I deleted apps that didn't serve me.

These small changes had a big impact. I felt less scattered. More focused. More in control. I reclaimed my time—not just in hours, but in presence. I could sit with a thought without needing to share it. I could enjoy a moment without documenting it. I could be with someone without splitting my attention.

Creativity returned. Ideas flowed more freely. I had space to think, to dream, to connect dots. I wrote again—not just for work, but for joy. I painted. I listened to music. I rediscovered parts of myself that had been waiting beneath the noise.

Of course, there were challenges. The world doesn't pause when you do. I missed emails, updates, and moments of news. But I learned to trust that I didn't need to be online constantly to stay informed. That I didn't need to respond immediately to be responsible. That I didn't need to be always available to be valuable.

I also learned to sit with discomfort. Silence can be hard. When we remove distractions, we're left with ourselves—our thoughts, our feelings, our questions. But that's where healing begins. That's where clarity lives. That's where we remember who we are.

I began sharing my experience. Some people were curious. Some were skeptical. A few were afraid. They'd say, "I could never do that." "I need my phone for work." "I'd feel disconnected." I understood. These devices are woven into our lives. They're tools, lifelines, companions. But they're also doors. And sometimes, stepping away helps us remember what's real.

I encouraged people to start small. One hour. One evening. One day. To notice how it feels. To observe their habits. To reclaim their choices. Many did. They slept better. They had deeper conversations. They felt more peace. Less reactivity. More intention. More presence.

Digital detox isn't a one-time fix. It's a rhythm. A way of living. It's about making space for what matters. To connect. To create. To be clear. It's about choosing presence over performance. Depth over distraction. Being over doing.

I still use technology. I still check my phone. I still scroll sometimes. But now I do it with intention. I know when to stop. When to pause. When to return to myself.

To me, that's the heart of digital detox. It's not about scarcity—it's about freedom. It's about remembering that your time is sacred. That your attention is powerful. That your presence is enough.

You don't have to disappear. You don't have to disconnect completely. You just have to choose. To reclaim. To begin again.

In a world that profits from your distraction, focus is resistance. Presence is power.

After just one weekend away from screens, my sleep improved. I fell asleep faster, stayed asleep longer, and woke up feeling refreshed. That's no coincidence. Harvard Medical School (2023) notes that blue light suppresses melatonin, the hormone that regulates sleep. And scrolling or streaming keeps the brain active when it should be winding down.

I also noticed better concentration. Tasks like writing, reading, and cooking—once overwhelming—became manageable. I wasn't multitasking. I wasn't checking my phone every few minutes. I was present. That presence led to flow, where time slowed and my mind fully engaged.

This isn't just anecdotal. Neuroscience shows that constant digital stimulation rewires the brain's reward system. Each notification triggers a dopamine release, reinforcing the habit. We crave novelty, even when it fragments our focus and drains our energy (APA, 2023).

That's why detox isn't just about turning off devices—it's about retraining the brain. It's about breaking compulsive loops and rediscovering the joy of sustained attention. It's about choosing depth over distraction.

It's interesting that 80% of U.S. smartphone users say they've made their own rules to limit screen time, but only 12% actually use the built-in screen time features (ElectroIQ, 2025). That space tells a story. We know we need limits, but it's hard to make sure they are followed. That's where being intentional comes in.

I started making simple rules for myself. No screens while eating. Don't bring your phone into the bedroom. No social media until noon. These weren't punishments; they were invitations. Invitations to be more aware of my food, my thoughts, and my mornings. And they worked. Not perfectly, but all the time.

I also learned how to enjoy being bored. That might sound strange, but being bored can help you be creative. Our minds start to wander, imagine, and connect dots when we aren't constantly stimulated. I got some of my best ideas when I was walking or staring out the window without headphones. That mental space is hard to find in a world full of content, but it's very good for you.

Digital detox looks different for everyone, of course. For some, it's a full retreat, with no devices for days or weeks. For some, it's a daily habit to spend an hour without screens every night. It's the intention that counts. The option to stop. To start over. To get back.

This is also something that workplaces are starting to see. Some businesses now promote tech-free times, limit access to email after hours, or even let employees leave their devices at work. These changes aren't just about getting more done; they're also about feeling better. About making spaces where mental health and focus are important.

I've seen how it affects my life. My relationships got stronger. My creativity grew. I felt less anxious. I felt more connected, but not to a network. I felt more connected to myself.

That's the main point of a digital detox. It's not about saying no to technology. It's important to remember that we are more than just our devices. That our attention is holy. That our brains need a break.

This is your invitation if you feel scattered, overwhelmed, or disconnected. Get away. Take a breath. Pay attention. Get your focus back. Take back your presence. Take back your life.

God is not far away. He's close. He is talking. He is waiting. And your mind—tired, wired, and wonderful—is ready to sleep. Your heart is ready to be whole. It's been distracted, divided, and devoted.

Stop holding on to the scroll. Lean into the quiet. Get your focus back. And let the Spirit show you the way home.

THE FORGOTTEN RESET TOOLS

Sleep, Nutrition, & Brain Health

At one point in my life, I thought resetting my brain meant doing something big—like taking a break from work, going on a retreat, or starting a new hobby. I believed change had to be dramatic to matter. But over time, I learned that some of the best ways to clear my mind and strengthen my emotions were already close by. They weren't flashy. They didn't cost much. They were simple: sleep, eat, and move. These basic things, often overlooked, are the quiet builders of brain health.

The first time I truly felt the effects of sleep deprivation was when I was a kid. It wasn't just tiredness—it was fog. I couldn't focus. My emotions were all over the place. I was irritable, forgetful, and disconnected. Back then, I thought it was just stress. But I noticed a big change when I started prioritizing sleep: going to bed at the same time every night, avoiding screens in the evening, and following a calming routine. I could think more clearly. My mood improved. I felt like myself again.

Sleep isn't just a break—it's restoration. The brain strengthens memories, clears toxins, and resets neural circuits while we sleep. Perrault et al. (2025) describe sleep as multidimensional, encompassing duration, quality, timing, and individual differences. Their research identified five sleep-biopsychosocial profiles, each linked to distinct patterns of brain connectivity and mental health outcomes.

For example, individuals with insufficient sleep were more prone to depression, anxiety, and stress, while those who slept well demonstrated better emotional regulation—even under pressure.

This study shows that sleep isn't one-size-fits-all. Some people function well on less sleep, while others need more to maintain mental and emotional balance. What matters is quality and consistency. Disrupted sleep, especially in midlife, is associated with accelerated cerebral aging and memory decline (Medical News Today, 2025). These findings underscore sleep's role as a daily reset for both body and mind.

Food is also vital for brain health. I used to eat whatever was convenient—sugary drinks, processed snacks, and late-night takeout. I didn't think much about how food affected my mind. But I noticed a difference when I began eating more whole foods: leafy greens, berries, nuts, and omega-3-rich fish. I had more energy. I became more focused. My mood lifted.

The brain consumes about 20% of the body's total energy. It thrives on nutrients that support neurotransmitter function, reduce inflammation, and promote neuroplasticity. The Mediterranean diet—rich in antioxidants, healthy fats, and fiber—has been linked to improved brain function and reduced risk of neurodegenerative diseases (Medical News Today, 2025).

Chanelle DeGraff (2025), a clinical nutritionist, emphasizes the importance of personalized nutrition plans. She notes that gut health, stable blood sugar, and adequate micronutrient intake all influence brain performance. For instance, deficiencies in B vitamins, magnesium, and vitamin D can impair mood and cognition. Conversely, regular consumption of fatty fish and flaxseeds boosts memory and emotional well-being.

Cutting back on sugar was one of the most transformative changes I made. Daniel, my gym partner who trained me for about a year, encouraged me to reduce all sugars—even carbs. I didn't realize how much it affected my mood until I made the switch. The headaches, mood swings, and brain fog all improved. I replaced sugary snacks with fruit, nuts, and dark chocolate. It wasn't deprivation—it was nourishment.

Hydration is also essential. About 75% of the brain is water, and even mild dehydration can impair attention, memory, and mood. I started carrying a water bottle and adding lemon or cucumber for flavour. Making hydration part of my daily routine was a small change with a big impact.

The Bible shows a very connected view of human health. Sleep, nutrition, and mental clarity are all parts of a bigger spiritual rhythm, not separate issues. Sleep is more than just rest; it shows that you trust someone.

When David says in Psalm 4:8, "*In peace I will lie down and sleep, for you alone, Lord, make me dwell in safety,*" he is giving up a lot. We trust that God is watching over us while we sleep, even when we are at our most vulnerable.

Proverbs 3:24 backs this up by saying that those who live without fear and walk in wisdom will have sweet sleep. "*The sleep of a laborer is sweet,*" says Ecclesiastes 5:12. This means that being honest and happy can make you feel better in both your body and mind. These verses don't just say that sleep is good; they also say that it is a spiritual practice based on trust, peace, and humility.

People treat nutrition with the same care. God has always given us food in a planned and generous way. In Genesis 1:29, He gives people **"every seed-bearing plant"** to eat, which is a natural and holy way to eat. Food is more than just fuel; it's a gift that shows how much God loves and cares for us. In 1 Corinthians 10:31,

Paul says, **"So whether you eat or drink or do anything else, do it all for the glory of God."** This verse makes us think differently about our daily habits by showing us how they can be ways to worship. Even eating can be a way to honor God. Proverbs also gives us good advice by telling us not to overdo it or give in to our wants. **"Do not join those who drink too much wine or eat too much meat,"** says chapter 23, verses 20–21.

These warnings aren't just about your health; they're also about being able to control yourself, knowing what's right and wrong, and living with purpose. The Bible has a lot to say about food. Being thankful, taking care of what we have, and giving what we have to others are all parts of it.

Mental and emotional health, though not explicitly defined in modern psychological terminology, is essential to biblical doctrine. According to Romans 12:2, we need to change by changing the way we think. This means giving up old ways of thinking and trusting God's wisdom.

This renewal affects both our minds and our spirits; it changes how we think, feel, and act in the world. Isaiah 26:3 says, **"You will keep in perfect peace those whose minds are steadfast, because they trust in you."** This verse is comforting for people who are feeling mentally stressed. Trust is a steadying force that helps the mind stay calm. Philippians 4:8 is a mental filter that tells Christians to focus on things that are true, good, fair, pure, beautiful, and worthy of praise.

This isn't just moral advice; it's also a way to be strong and clear-headed. "***Above all else, guard your heart, for everything you do flows from it***" (Proverbs 4:23) says it all. The Bible says that the heart is where we think, feel, and want to do things. Guarding our inner world means being careful about what we let change it.

These verses together make a tapestry of wisdom that shows how important it is to eat well, get enough sleep, and keep your mind clear. They remind us that our bodies and minds are not separate from our spiritual lives. God made them and keeps them alive through His grace. Sleep is a way to feel better, food is a sign of having enough, and thought is a way to change. When we take care of these parts of ourselves, we are not only trying to be healthy; we are also following a divine pattern of wholeness.

We should treat our bodies and minds like sacred gifts, according to the Bible. Food, sleep, and mental clarity are not just things we need for our bodies; they are also things we need for our spirits. They show how much we care about things, how much we trust God, and how much we want to live wisely and well. We honour the Creator who made us whole by taking care of these parts of our health.

Movement, though not the central focus of this chapter, deserves mention. Exercise increases blood flow to the brain, enhances neurotrophic factors, and boosts mood through endorphin release. Even light movement—walking, stretching, dancing—can sharpen thinking and support emotional resilience.

Sleep, nutrition, and exercise work together to sustain brain health. They are the reset tools we often overlook. They're simple, accessible, and powerful. Yet in our fast-paced world, they're frequently neglected. We sacrifice sleep for productivity. We choose convenience over nourishment. We sit for hours. And we wonder why we feel foggy, anxious, or disconnected.

I've seen these tools transform lives. One woman struggled with anxiety and poor sleep. She had tried everything—therapy, medication, meditation—but nothing worked. A lifestyle review revealed she slept only five hours a night, skipped meals, and relied heavily on coffee.

We started with small steps: a consistent bedtime, a nourishing breakfast, and a daily walk. Within weeks, her anxiety eased. Her sleep improved. She felt hopeful again.

A college student came to me with brain fog and fatigue. His diet consisted mostly of processed foods, and he stayed up late, fueled by energy drinks. We created a simple meal plan with whole grains, lean protein, and vegetables, and established a sleep schedule. He became more alert, focused, and vibrant.

These stories are common. They remind us that the brain is responsive. It listens to how we treat it. It adapts. It heals. But it needs support.

The World Health Organization (WHO) and the Food and Agriculture Organization (FAO) of the United Nations recently released new guidelines for brain and metabolic health. They recommend increasing intake of whole grains, legumes, fruits, and vegetables, while reducing processed foods, trans fats, and added sugars (Medical News Today, 2025). These guidelines aren't just about physical health—they're about mental sharpness.

Nutrition plays a crucial role. The gut-brain axis—the communication network between the gut and central nervous system—is vital for mental health. The gut produces about 90% of the body's serotonin, a neurotransmitter that regulates mood (O'Mahony et al., 2015). A diet rich in fiber, fermented foods, and diverse plants supports a healthy gut microbiome, which in turn enhances mood and reduces anxiety.

A significant study found that individuals following a Mediterranean-style diet—abundant in vegetables, fruits, whole grains, legumes, and healthy fats—had significantly lower rates of depression compared to those consuming a Western diet high in processed foods and sugar (Jacka et al., 2017). This isn't just correlation; randomized controlled trials confirm causation.

Omega-3 fatty acids are excellent for brain health. Found in fatty fish like salmon and sardines, they strengthen neuronal membranes and reduce inflammation. Low omega-3 levels are linked to increased risk of depression, ADHD, and cognitive decline (Grosso et al., 2014). Supplementation has shown promise in improving mood and attention in both children and adults.

Micronutrients matter too. Deficiencies in B vitamins—especially B6, B12, and folate—can impair neurotransmitter synthesis, leading to fatigue, irritability, and forgetfulness (Kennedy, 2016). Stress and poor diet can deplete magnesium, essential for over 300 enzymatic reactions, including those involved in brain signaling. Low magnesium levels are associated with anxiety and sleep disturbances (Boyle et al., 2017).

Vitamin D, often called the "sunshine vitamin," is also critical. It regulates immune function and inflammation, and low levels are linked to depression and cognitive deficits (Anglin et al., 2013). In Canada and other northern regions with limited winter sunlight, supplementation may be necessary to maintain optimal levels.

Hydration, though often overlooked, is vital. Losing just 1–2% of body water can impair cognition, mood, and focus (Ganio et al., 2011). The brain is highly sensitive to fluid balance, and adequate hydration supports alertness and memory.

Sleep hygiene is equally important. Experts recommend maintaining a consistent sleep schedule, creating a calming bedtime routine, limiting screen time before bed, and ensuring a dark, quiet sleep environment.

These habits support melatonin production and regulate circadian rhythms (Harvard Medical School, 2023).

I've integrated these habits into my own life. I read before bed, dim the lights in the evening, and avoid screens after 10 p.m. I wake up at the same time daily, even on weekends. I eat foods that nourish and energize me. I move my body because I enjoy it—not because I have to. And I feel the difference—not just in energy, but in clarity, creativity, and self-connection.

Remember, deep sleep triggers glymphatic clearance, which removes neurotoxins like beta-amyloid—linked to Alzheimer's disease (Xie et al., 2013). This nightly cleansing is essential for long-term brain health. Without sufficient sleep, these toxins accumulate, increasing the risk of cognitive decline.

Sleep also consolidates memory. During sleep, the hippocampus communicates with the neocortex to transfer short-term memories into long-term storage. This process is most active during slow-wave and REM sleep (Diekelmann & Born, 2010). Sleep deprivation impairs learning and emotional regulation.

Chronic sleep deprivation has even been linked to a smaller prefrontal cortex—the brain region responsible for emotion regulation, decision-making, and impulse control (Krause et al., 2017). So lack of sleep doesn't just make us tired—it undermines our ability to cope, solve problems, and connect with others.

These tools aren't very pretty. They won't spread like a virus. But they do work. They are the basis of cognitive performance, mental health, and emotional strength. They are the buttons we need to start over. If you're feeling anxious, foggy, or disconnected, this is the place to start. Sleep. Feed. Go.

Not quite right. Not all at once. But all the time. Not too hard. With love. When we talk about resetting the brain, we often think of meditation, therapy, or taking a break from technology. All of these are good tools. But sleep, food, and exercise are the biological foundations of mental clarity. They aren't just helpful; they're necessary.

Even the best psychological strategies have a hard time working without them. Exercise makes blood flow to the brain faster, which brings oxygen and nutrients. It also makes the brain release brain-derived neurotrophic factor (BDNF), a protein that helps the brain change and make new connections (Szuhany et al., 2015).

Regular exercise has been shown to help with executive function, make depression less severe, and protect against cognitive decline that comes with age. Even a little bit of activity, like walking quickly for 30 minutes a day, can have big benefits.

A meta-analysis of more than 100 studies revealed that aerobic exercise enhances attention, processing speed, and working memory in individuals of all ages (Smith et al., 2010). For older adults, engaging in physical activity is one of the most effective means of preserving cognitive health.

Sleep, nutrition, and movement work together to make a synergistic triad. They affect each other. If you don't sleep well, you might want to eat sugary foods. Not getting enough nutrients in your diet can make it hard to sleep. Not moving around can make you feel bad and slow down digestion.

The brain works best when all three are in sync. I've seen this change happen in my life and in the lives of my clients. A woman who was having trouble with brain fog and a low mood started a simple routine: going to bed and waking up at the same time every day, eating a Mediterranean-style diet, and going for walks every day. Her energy came back in a few weeks. Her mind felt clearer. She said it was like "waking up from a long fog."

Another client, a high-level executive, was getting burned out. He was glued to his desk, sleeping only five hours a night, and missing meals. We began with the basics, like how to get enough sleep, eat healthy meals, and take breaks to move around.

Not only did his productivity come back, it shot up. He was more focused, more creative, and more present. These stories are not unusual. They remind us that the brain and body are not two separate things. What we eat, how we sleep, and how we move all help it grow. We make it possible for healing, growth, and clarity to happen when we respect these rhythms.

MINDFULNESS AND MEDITATION

REBOOTING YOUR MENTAL OPERATING SYSTEM

There was a season in my life when my mind felt like a browser with too many tabs open. Thoughts raced. Worries piled up. I'd wake up already tired, my heart heavy with the weight of unfinished tasks and unspoken fears. I tried to push through, to be productive, to stay strong. But deep down, I knew I wasn't okay. My soul was cluttered. My spirit was weary. And I longed for peace—not just quiet, but the kind of peace that settles deep in your bones.

That's when I began to explore mindfulness and meditation—not as trendy practices, but as sacred rhythms. Not as escapes, but as invitations. I didn't find them in a wellness app or a yoga studio. I found them in Scripture. In the quiet places where God speaks. In the stillness where His presence meets our chaos.

One morning, I sat with my Bible open to Psalm 46. The words felt like a whisper: *"Be still, and know that I am God"* (Psalm 46:10, ESV). I had read that verse a hundred times before, but that day it landed differently. It wasn't a suggestion. It was a command. A lifeline. A call to stop striving and start trusting. To be still—not just physically, but mentally, emotionally, spiritually.

So I began practicing stillness. I'd wake up early, before the world stirred, and sit in silence. I'd breathe slowly, intentionally, and repeat that verse like a prayer: *Be still. Know. God.* At first, my mind resisted. It wandered. It worried. But I kept returning. And slowly, the noise began to fade. I began to hear the quiet voice of God—not in thunder, but in the whisper (1 Kings 19:12).

Mindfulness, in its truest form, is about presence. It's about being fully here, fully aware, fully surrendered. And Scripture is full of invitations to live this way. Jesus Himself modeled it. He often withdrew to lonely places to pray (Luke 5:16). He didn't rush. He didn't multitask. He was present—with the Father, with people, with Himself.

I remember one afternoon when I was overwhelmed by a decision I had to make. I couldn't think clearly. I was torn between fear and faith. So I stepped outside, sat under a tree, and opened to Philippians 4. The words wrapped around me like a blanket: *"Do not be anxious about anything, but in everything by prayer and supplication with thanksgiving let your requests be made known to God. And the peace of God, which surpasses all understanding, will guard your hearts and your minds in Christ Jesus"* (Philippians 4:6–7, ESV).

I began to breathe those words in. I named my fears. I thanked God for His presence. I surrendered the outcome. And in that moment, I felt a shift—not in my circumstances, but in my spirit. Peace came. Not because I had figured everything out, but because I had handed it over.

Meditation, in the biblical sense, is not emptying the mind—it's filling it with truth. Psalm 1 describes the person who delights in the law of the Lord and meditates on it day and night. *"He is like a tree planted by streams of water, which yields its fruit in season and whose leaf does not wither"* (Psalm 1:2–3, NIV). That image stayed with me. I wanted to be that tree—rooted, nourished, resilient.

So I began to meditate on Scripture. Not just read it, but dwell in it. I'd take one verse and carry it through the day. I'd repeat it during moments of stress. I'd write it on sticky notes and place them where I'd see them. Over time, those words became anchors. They grounded me. They guided me. They reminded me who I was and whose I was.

One of the most transformative practices I adopted was breath prayer. It's simple: you pair your breath with a short prayer. Inhale: *"Lord Jesus Christ."* Exhale: *"Have mercy on me."* Or inhale: *"You are my peace."* Exhale: *"I trust You."* These prayers became rhythms. They helped me stay connected to God throughout the day. They turned ordinary moments into sacred ones.

I also began to notice how mindfulness helped me love others better. When I was present, I listened more deeply. I responded more gently. I saw people—not just their needs, but their hearts. Jesus did this so beautifully. He saw the woman at the well. He noticed the bleeding woman in the crowd. He paused for children. He was never too busy to be present.

Mindfulness and meditation, rooted in Scripture, have become my spiritual reset. They help me clear the clutter, quiet the noise, and return to the One who holds all things together. They remind me that I don't have to carry everything. That I can cast my cares on Him, because He cares for me (1 Peter 5:7).

There are still days when my mind feels crowded. When anxiety creeps in. When I forget to pause. But now I know how to return. I know how to reboot. I know how to be still.

And in that stillness, I find God. Not just in the mountaintop moments, but in the ordinary ones. In the breath. In the silence. In the Word.

There's a quiet miracle that happens when we slow down. When we stop rushing, stop reacting, stop trying to control everything. In that stillness, we begin to hear again—not just the noise of our thoughts, but the voice of God. For years, I lived in a state of mental hurry. My mind was always multitasking, always planning, always bracing for the next thing. I thought that was strength. I thought that was faith. But it was exhaustion. And it wasn't until I began practicing biblical mindfulness and meditation that I realized how much I had been missing.

Mindfulness, in its biblical essence, is about being fully here, fully aware, fully surrendered to the moment God has given. It's not about emptying the mind—it's about filling it with truth. Psalm 119:15 says, *"I will meditate on your precepts and fix my eyes on your ways"* (ESV). That's not passive. That's intentional. It's a choice to dwell in God's Word, to anchor our thoughts in His promises, to let His truth shape our inner world.

I began this journey in a season of deep anxiety and depression back in 2017. I was overwhelmed by decisions, responsibilities, and the weight of uncertainty. I'd pray, but my prayers felt rushed. I'd read Scripture, but my mind would wander. I longed for peace, but I didn't know how to access it. One morning, I read Isaiah 26:3: *"You keep him in perfect peace whose mind is stayed on you, because he trusts in you"* (ESV). That phrase—*whose mind is stayed on you*—became my invitation. I didn't need to fix everything. I needed to fix my mind on Him.

So I started small. Five minutes of silence. Breathing deeply. Repeating a verse. Listening. Not for answers, but for presence. And slowly, my mind began to settle. The racing thoughts quieted. The fear loosened its grip. I wasn't just calming my nervous system—I was communing with God.

Meditation, in Scripture, is often tied to remembrance. In Joshua 1:8, God tells Joshua, *"This Book of the Law shall not depart from your mouth, but you shall meditate on it day and night, so that you may be careful to do according to all that is written in it. For then you will make your way prosperous, and then you will have good success"* (ESV). Meditation isn't just reflection—it's transformation. It's allowing God's Word to shape our decisions, our reactions, our identity.

I began carrying verses with me throughout the day. I'd write them on index cards, place them on my mirror, keep them in my pocket. When anxiety flared, I'd pull one out and breathe it in. *"Cast all your anxiety on Him because He cares for you"* (1 Peter 5:7, NIV). That verse became a lifeline. Not just a comfort, but a practice. I'd imagine myself handing my worries to Jesus, one by one, like stones I no longer needed to carry.

There were days I didn't feel like meditating. Days when the noise was loud and the silence felt unreachable. But I learned that showing up matters. That even when my mind wandered, God didn't. He was there, waiting, whispering, loving. Psalm 139 reminds us that we can't escape His presence. *"Where shall I go from your Spirit? Or where shall I flee from your presence?"* (Psalm 139:7, ESV). That truth became my anchor. I didn't need to perform. I just needed to be.

Over time, these practices became part of my spiritual rhythm. Not a checklist, but a lifeline. I'd begin my day with silence, Scripture, and breath. I'd pause throughout the day to reconnect. I'd end my day with gratitude and reflection. And my mind—once cluttered and chaotic—began to feel like a sanctuary.

I still have anxious thoughts. I still get distracted. But now I know how to return. I know how to reboot. I know how to be still and know.

Mindfulness and meditation, when rooted in Scripture, are not self-help—they're soul-help. They're not about escaping reality—they're about entering it with God. They're not about controlling our thoughts—they're about surrendering them.

So if your mind feels overwhelmed, if your spirit feels weary, if your heart longs for peace—start here. Be still. Breathe. Meditate on truth. Invite God into the quiet.

THE BEGINNNING OF A SHIFT

Novelty - Trying New Things

There was a time in my life when every day felt like a copy of the one before. Wake up, check my phone, rush through breakfast or skip breakfast, rush to work at an intensive mental health unit, sit at my desk, answer emails, eat lunch at the same spot, drive the same route home. I wasn't unhappy exactly, but I felt dull. Like my mind had lost its spark. I was functioning, but not flourishing. And I couldn't figure out why.

Then one weekend, almost by accident, I signed up at a gym. I had never touched weights before. I didn't know the difference of weights and cables and what body parts to work out. But something in me said, "Try it, watch others and get a routine developed." So I did. I showed up, awkward and unsure, and sat at some of the machines which I had to figure out how to use and begin to explore the different options of working out different body parts. My first attempts showed little to no progress. I did not know how much weight to lift, and how to do it properly. But I laughed. I felt alive. I felt something I hadn't felt in a long time—curiosity.

That was the beginning of a shift that became a lifestyle for me. I met others who would share their work out plan with me as I became more determined.

I started reading about the brain and learned something that changed everything: novelty lights up the mind. When we try something new, our brain releases dopamine—the feel-good neurotransmitter that fuels motivation, learning, and joy. It's the same chemical that fires when we fall in love, win a prize, or hear our favourite song. But here's the beautiful part: we don't need grand adventures to trigger it. We just need change. A new experience. A fresh challenge.

I began experimenting with new experiences. I took a different route to work and tried Ethiopian, Greek, Russian, Ghanaian, Hakha, and many other ethnic foods for the first time. I learned to play a few chords on both the guitar and piano. I joined a dance class with my wife Kathleen, who was seven months pregnant at the time. I started writing books and even entered a singing competition called *Gospel Challenge*, where I made it to the top eleven contestants. I went to job interviews just for the fun of it, began taking cruises, and vacationed in various locations. I also started going on mission trips to different countries and embarked on many new adventures—like visiting Machu Picchu in Peru, hiking through jungles and volcanoes in Hawaii, and snorkeling in tropical waters.

Each new experience felt like a breath of fresh air for my brain. I felt more alert, more engaged, and more present.

One afternoon, I found myself hiking a trail I'd never explored. The path was uneven, the trees unfamiliar, the sounds different. I had to pay attention—to where I stepped, to what I heard, to how I felt.

That's when I realized: novelty demands presence. When we do something new, we can't rely on autopilot. We have to show up. And that presence is what recharges us. I've noticed this in other people as well. A friend of mine, who had been in the same job for years and was stuck in a rut, decided to take a painting class. He hadn't painted since high school, but his energy changed in just a few weeks. He was happier, more confident, and more open. It wasn't about becoming an artist; it was about waking up.

Trying new things also makes you stronger. We learn to adapt better when we do things that are outside our comfort zone. We learn to deal with uncertainty, accept flaws, and grow through pain. After my son Jadon and I came back from Thailand, I remember learning how to make Thai food from scratch. I burned the rice. The curry was too hot. But I laughed. I learned. I gave it another shot. And every time, my brain changed—not just to cook, but to keep going.

This is also based on science. Novelty fuels neuroplasticity, which is the brain's ability to change and adapt. We make new neural pathways when we do things we've never done before, especially when they push us. We make connections stronger. We make our brains more flexible. Instead of weights, you use curiosity to work out your brain.

I started to notice how my mood changed when I tried new things. I wasn't as worried. Not as stuck. More hopeful. It felt like my mind had been waiting for me to change things up. To shock it. To give it something new to eat.

Even small changes made a difference. Listening to a different kind of music. Moving my furniture around. Writing in a café instead of at home. Every shift was a spark. And a lot of sparks can start a fire again.

I also learned that new things made my relationships stronger. When I asked my friends to do something new with me—like go to a sports game, an escape room, a painting class, or a magic show—we became closer in ways I didn't expect. We laughed. We fell. We found out. And those things we did together became memories that stuck.

One of the most powerful times in my life was when I volunteered at a prison for young offenders. I had never done volunteer work before. I didn't know how to tell the difference between a criminal and a saint. But I did show up every day I was supposed to. I got myself with a prisoner who was supposed to be with me. I paid attention. And in that space, with strangers who had broken the law all around me, I felt connected—to their loneliness, their regret, their judgment, and to myself.

It's not always easy to try new things. It can be strange, uncomfortable, or even scary. But it's also exciting. It reminds us that we can grow. That our routines don't define us. We can surprise ourselves.

Some days still feel like they repeat. But I know how to stop the cycle now. I know how to get my energy back. I know how to agree to something I don't know. And every time I do, my brain says thank you.

That made me want to learn more about the science of novelty and brain health. I found out that trying new things is not only fun, but it also helps the body heal. When something new happens, it activates the brain's reward system, which releases dopamine. This makes you more motivated, helps you learn, and makes you more emotionally strong (Krebs et al., 2009). It's the same chemical that makes you happy, curious, and want to learn new things.

We stimulate neuroplasticity—the brain's ability to form new neural connections and adapt to change (Draganski et al., 2006)—when we try new things, especially ones that push us. This means that every time we try something new, we are literally changing the way our brains work.

We're making our brains more flexible, our memories better, and our emotional control stronger.

One study discovered that participating in novel activities can improve working memory and executive function, particularly in older adults (Park et al., 2014). The researchers urged participants to acquire digital photography and quilting skills, which required prolonged focus and problem-solving abilities. After a few weeks, participants who did more active things showed big improvements in their thinking skills compared to those who did less active things.

This study really spoke to me. I always thought that stress or getting older made you less mentally sharp. But now I knew that the brain works best when it is challenged. It wants to get bigger. It wants to be shocked.

Even little changes made a difference. I began writing books in a coffee shop, in an airplane when I travel to conferences, instead of at home. Instead of my usual playlists, I listened to jazz. I read books that aren't in my favorite genres. These changes didn't take much work, but they made room for new ideas, feelings, and points of view.

Doing new things also helped me deal with my anxiety. When I was stuck in thought loops that kept going around and around, new things helped me break the cycle. They gave my mind something new to think about.

A study demonstrated that novelty can alleviate stress by enhancing positive affect and diminishing rumination (Gerrig & McKoon, 2001). In other words, trying new things helps us stop worrying and start being involved.

There is also proof that new things can make you more creative. When we encounter novel stimuli, we stimulate divergent thinking—the capacity to produce various solutions to a problem (Fink et al., 2009). That's why artists, writers, and inventors often look for new places to work. It's not just inspiration; it's brain science.

I started to see new things as food. Our brains need different kinds of experiences just like our bodies need different kinds of food. We stop moving forward without it. We do well with it.

It's not always easy to try new things, of course. It can be uncomfortable, scary, or even annoying. But that pain is a part of growing. It teaches us to be okay with not knowing everything, to accept flaws, and to be strong.

One thing I learned is that new things don't have to be big. They can be soft. A new way to cook. A new way to walk. Talking to someone you don't usually talk to. These little changes add up. They give things a push. They remind us that we can change.

If you're feeling stuck, tired, or uninspired, do something different. It doesn't have to be huge. Just not the same. Your brain is waiting. It comes to life when you give it something new.

EMOTIONAL RESET

LETTING GO OF TOXIC THOUGHT PATTERNS

When I tried to sit in silence, I didn't realize how loud my inner critic had gotten. I had made a quiet space for myself, with no phone or other things to keep me busy—just me and my thoughts. But instead of peace, I got a lot of bad news. *"You're not doing enough."* *"You always screw things up."* *"Why can't you be more like them*?" It never stopped. And it wasn't coming from anyone else; it was coming from me.

At that point, I knew that something had to change.

Thought patterns that are harmful don't always show up right away. They come in quietly, pretending to be self-control, caution, or realism. They remind us of things we've heard in the past, things we're afraid of now, and things we're unsure about in the future. They change the way we see ourselves, the way we treat other people, and the way we move through the world over time.

I thought these thoughts were just a part of who I was—that being hard on myself was the cost of getting better. But the truth is, toxic thoughts don't help—they hurt. They don't inspire; they freeze. And they don't keep you safe; they cut you off.

It's not about pretending everything is okay when you let go of these patterns. It's about choosing a different lens. It's about stopping the cycle and asking yourself, "*Is this thought helping or hurting me?*"

Noticing was one of the first things I did. Not making a judgment—just noticing. I would catch myself thinking, "*I'm not good enough,*" and instead of getting upset, I would stop and say, "*There it is again.*" That simple act of being aware made space. Room to ask questions. Room to make a choice.

I started writing in a journal not to change myself, but to learn more about myself. I'd write down the bad thoughts and then try to prove them wrong. "*Is this real?*" "*Where did this come from?*" "*What would I say to a friend who felt this way?*" That last question was really strong. I refused to give myself compassion, even though I knew I was giving it to others.

I also began to talk to myself in a way that was based on truth—not empty affirmations, but reminders grounded in reality. "*You can take a break.*" "*Making mistakes is part of learning.*" "*You are worthy of love, even when things are hard.*" It was strange at first. But as time went on, those words started to feel like home.

I've learned that a lot of the bad thoughts I had were ways I had learned to deal with pain, rejection, or fear. They had a purpose at one point. But now they were keeping me stuck.

Letting go also meant letting myself off the hook—for the times I believed the lies, for the times I didn't say anything, for the times I let fear take over. It's not enough to forgive someone once; you have to do it over and over again. And every time I chose it, I felt better.

I started to be around people who made me feel good—books, podcasts, and friends who spoke life instead of shame. I took care of my surroundings like a garden, pulling out weeds, planting seeds, and helping things grow.

One of the most healing things that happened to me was when I started meditating on the Word of God—not to get away from my thoughts, but to watch them, get them into my spirit. I would sit quietly, take deep breaths, and watch my thoughts like clouds moving across the sky, and the Word of God replaced them. Some were dark thoughts, but God's Word always cancelled them out. A few were light. But none of them lasted. That understanding set me free. I wasn't what I thought. I was the one who was watching them.

I also leaned into being thankful. Toxic thoughts often dwell on absence—what's lacking, what's amiss, what's fractured. Thankfulness changes how you see things, helping you notice abundance. At the end of each day, I would say three things I was thankful for. It was hard some days. But even on the worst days, there was always something— a hot meal, a kind word, or a laugh.

It doesn't mean that toxic thought patterns won't come back after you let them go. It means they don't get to make the final decision anymore. We've made new paths based on truth, kindness, and hope.

There are still times when the old thoughts come back to me. But now I know what to say. I know how to stop, take a breath, and choose a new story. I know how to start over.

And that reset isn't just emotional; it's also spiritual. It's taking back the voice God gave me—the one that says, "*You are fearfully and wonderfully made*" (Psalm 139:14). The one that says, "*There is no condemnation for those who are in Christ Jesus*" (Romans 8:1). The one that says, "*You are loved with an everlasting love*" (Jeremiah 31:3).

Start here if your mind is heavy, your thoughts are harsh, or your heart is tired. Pay attention. Challenge. Change. Let go. Surround. Take a deep breath. Start over. You are not the bad thoughts you have. You are the one who can let them go.

Living with toxic thought patterns can make you suffer in a quiet way. You can't always see it. It doesn't always show up in big fights or public outbursts. Sometimes, it just slowly takes away your happiness— a constant buzzing of self-doubt, a weight in the chest that never goes away. I know this because I've been there.

For years, I had thoughts that weren't mine. *"You're too much." "You don't have enough." "You'll never change."* These weren't true; they were echoes. Criticism, rejection, and comparison echo. They had settled in my mind like squatters, and I didn't know how to get rid of them. I believed they were a part of me. But they weren't. They were patterns. And you can break patterns.

The first thing I did to reset my emotions was to see the pattern. It sounds easy, but it isn't. Toxic thoughts can sneak up on you. They wear a mask of reason. They sound like being careful, humble, and realistic. But they're really fear. Shame. Wounds from the past. I started to notice when my thoughts got mean. I'd stop and ask myself, *"Would I say this to someone I care about?"* The answer was usually no. That was my cue to question the idea.

Psychologists call this cognitive restructuring, which means changing distorted thoughts into more balanced ones. It is a fundamental aspect of cognitive behavioral therapy (Beck, 2011). But to me, it wasn't just a method—it was a way of getting closer to God. I started to tell the truth instead of lies. Not just any truth, but God's truth.

When my mind told me I was a failure, I remembered Romans 8:1, which says, *"**There is therefore now no condemnation for those who are in Christ Jesus**."* Psalm 139:14 helped me when I felt unworthy: *"**I praise you because I am fearfully and wonderfully made**."*

These verses weren't just meant to make you feel better; they were meant to correct you. They changed the way I think. They reminded me that my identity doesn't depend on how well I do things, how perfect I am, or how much people like me. It comes from grace.

I also learned that unmet emotional needs can lead to toxic thoughts. When I felt like no one loved me, it was usually because I was alone. I felt like a burden because I didn't ask for help. Emotional reset meant taking care of those needs with kindness, not shame. I began to ask myself, "*What do I need right now?*" Sometimes the answer was rest. Sometimes connection. Sometimes silence. It helped me listen to myself.

Toxic thoughts are about what you don't have, what's wrong, or what's broken. Thankfulness changes how you see things, helping you notice abundance.

Setting limits was also part of letting go of harmful thought patterns. I had to stay away from voices that made the lies stronger. That meant unfollowing some people, spending less time with others, and choosing what I was around. I surrounded myself with people who spoke life— books, podcasts, and friends who reminded me who I really was.

One of the biggest changes happened when I started to forgive myself—for the times I believed the lies, for the times I didn't say anything, for the times I let fear take over. It's not enough to forgive someone once; you have to do it over and over again. And every time I chose it, I felt better.

I still think bad things. They still come. But now I know how to reach them. I know how to stop, take a breath, and choose a new story. I know how to start over.

So if your mind is heavy, your thoughts are harsh, or your heart is tired, start here. Pay attention. Challenge. Change. Let go. Surround. Take a deep breath. Start over.

You are not the bad thoughts you have. You are the only one who can let go.

THE POWER OF SILENCE

HOW QUIET TIME RESETS MENTAL OVERLOAD

For years, I filled every moment with noise: music playing in the background, podcasts playing while I cooked, notifications pinging on my phone, and conversations on top of thoughts that never stopped. I thought it was fine. I thought it was useful. But I started to feel the weight of it over time. My brain was tired—not just tired, but overloaded. It was like a computer with too many tabs open, getting slower and slower until it froze.

I remember one night when I got home from work, sat on the couch, and couldn't even decide what to eat. There was so much information in my head that even the simplest choices seemed impossible. I didn't feel like talking. I didn't want to scroll. I didn't want to have to think. I just wanted some peace and quiet.

I turned everything off. No music. No screens. No talking. I lit a candle, sat in the dark, and took a deep breath. At first, it was strange. It was even uncomfortable. I was trying to fill the silence with my thoughts. But I kept going. I let the quiet wrap around me like a blanket. And little by little, things changed. My shoulders fell. I took a deep breath. My head started to clear.

That was the start of my relationship with silence.

I began making time for peace and quiet every day. Not hours—just a few minutes. A walk without music. A morning without any screens. A break between jobs. And I noticed something amazing: the more quiet I let things be, the clearer my mind became. Thoughts that had been mixed up started to get clearer. Feelings that had been hidden began to come out. Choices that seemed impossible started to make sense.

Silence was like a reset button for me.

There is something holy about silence. It's where we find ourselves. It's where we hear the whispers that say, "*You're tired,*" "*You're enough,*" and "*You're not alone*" under the noise. We stop performing when we are quiet. We stop responding. We begin to pay attention.

I remember one afternoon when I sat by the lake, turned off my phone, and closed my journal. I just watched the water. The wind blew softly across the top. Birds sang from the trees. I felt something I hadn't felt in weeks—peace—in that stillness. Not the kind that comes from fixing things, but the kind that comes from letting them go.

This is what science says. Research indicates that silence may decrease cortisol levels, lower blood pressure, and enhance cognitive function (Kujala et al., 2021). When we stop being constantly stimulated, our brains go into a default mode network. This is a state that helps us think about things, remember things, and deal with our feelings. In other words, being quiet helps us get better.

But silence isn't just the lack of sound. It's about the space that is there. Room to think. Room to feel. Room to be.

I've seen this happen in my relationships as well. I started to listen more deeply when I stopped trying to fill every silence with words. I started to notice the pauses, the hesitations, and the feelings that were hidden. Being quiet made me a better friend. A better spouse. A better father. A better person.

It also helped me think of new things. Ideas came to me in the silence. People got to know each other. There was a lot of inspiration. I started writing again—but not just emails and lists. I wrote stories, poems, and reflections. In the quiet, I found parts of myself that I had forgotten about. I love writing and getting my thoughts on paper.

Of course, it's not always easy to be quiet. It can make you feel bad sometimes. It can show pain sometimes. But that's part of starting over. We make room for healing when we let ourselves sit with what is real. We stop blocking out pain. We begin to notice.

I started to see silence as a skill to learn. I didn't just happen upon it; I chose it. I would wake up and sit still before the day started. I would stop between meetings to take a breath. I'd end the day by thinking about things in peace. These times became anchors. They reminded me that I didn't have to keep up with the speed of the world. I could go at my own pace.

During a silent retreat, I had one of the most powerful experiences of my life. No talking. No cell phones. Nothing but nature, peace, and quiet. It was hard to get used to at first. My mind fought back. But on the second day, I really felt like I was there. I saw how the light changed as it went through the trees. I could feel how each breath felt. I could hear my heart beating. And in that quiet, I felt close to everything—including myself and God.

There was a time in my life when my mind was like a storm. Thoughts colliding with one another. Anxiety rising like waves. I was tired, overwhelmed, and spiritually dry. I prayed, but it felt like I was in a hurry. I read the Bible, but my mind started to wander. I wanted peace, but I didn't know how to get it.

Then, one morning, I opened my Bible to Psalm 62:5: "*For God alone, O my soul, wait in silence, for my hope is from him*" (ESV). That verse made me stop. Be quiet and wait. Not just wait. Not just pray. But wait quietly. It seemed like an invitation. A test. A lifeline.

I gave it a shot. I sat quietly—not to get anything done, but to be there. I didn't bring a list of things I wanted. I didn't try to fix anything. I just listened and breathed. At first, it didn't feel good. My mind was racing. I couldn't sit still. But I stayed. And slowly, the noise started to go away. My spirit started to calm down. And in that silence, I could feel God close by—not loud. Not dramatic, but profound.

There are many times in the Bible when God meets people in silence. God didn't speak to Elijah in the wind, the earthquake, or the fire. Instead, He spoke to him in a quiet whisper (1 Kings 19:12). Jesus didn't just talk about rest; He practiced it too. He knew that silence wasn't a choice—it was a must.

It's not often that we hear silence in our modern world. We are always getting information, stimulation, and noise thrown at us. But the Bible tells us that we find strength in stillness. "*Be still, and know that I am God*" (Psalm 46:10, ESV). That verse isn't just pretty; it's also useful. It tells you to stop trying, stop spinning, and start trusting.

Silent prayer was one of the most healing things I found. Not saying anything. Not asking. Just being with God. I would picture myself resting in His presence, like a child sleeping in their parent's lap. No words are needed. Just love.

Romans 8:26 says, "*Likewise the Spirit helps us in our weakness*." This is similar to this kind of prayer. We don't know what to pray for, but the Spirit Himself prays for us with groans that are too deep for words (ESV). At times, silence is the most sincere prayer we can give. And there, the Spirit meets us.

I also learned that being quiet helped me let go. Give up control. Don't be afraid. Stop feeling like I need to know everything. I remembered that I'm not God when it was quiet—and that made me feel better. I don't have to carry everything. I don't have to fix everything. I just have to be quiet and let Him be God.

Being quiet also helped me get my emotions back in order. When I was mad, being quiet helped me calm down. It let me feel when I was sad. It helped me enjoy the moment when I was happy. It became a mirror for my soul, showing me what was true, what was hidden, and what needed to be healed.

Jesus did this very well. He prayed all night before picking His disciples (Luke 6:12). He went to Gethsemane before going to the cross (Matthew 26:36). He took His time making decisions. He didn't shy away from pain. He met it in silence—with the Father.

I now believe that silence is one of the most important spiritual practices we can do. It's not showy. It doesn't get noticed. But it brings us closer to God. It gets rid of the junk. It makes the heart feel better. It makes the ears open.

And it's open to everyone. You don't need to go away. You don't need everything to be perfect. You only need a minute. A breath. A willingness to stop.

Step into the quiet if your mind is full, your spirit is tired, or your heart longs for peace. Make the noise quieter. Get your Bible out. Sit down with God.

There is something in silence. It has a lot of good ideas. It's a place where we remember who we are. That's where we start over. Start here if your mind is racing or your spirit is tired. Make the noise go away. Walk into the silence. Take a deep breath. Pay attention.

You don't have to fix everything. You don't have to figure it all out. You just need to be quiet.

And in that quiet, you'll see things more clearly. You'll find peace. You'll discover yourself.

RESETTING AFTER BURNOUT

STRATEGIES FOR MENTAL RECOVERY

I didn't realize I was burned out until I finally stopped moving. It wasn't a dramatic collapse—no ambulance, no tears—just a quiet unraveling. I found myself sitting at my desk after working ten hours, staring blankly at the screen, and suddenly became aware that I couldn't remember the last time I felt joy. Not excitement. Not even contentment. Just pure, unfiltered joy.

My body was fatigued, my mind clouded, and my spirit numb. I had been pushing through for so long—meeting deadlines, fulfilling expectations, carrying responsibilities—that I hadn't noticed I was running on empty. The emotional and cognitive exhaustion had crept in slowly, disguised as productivity and perseverance.

That night, I asked Kathleen and the children to pray for me. I sat on the edge of my bed, overwhelmed and unable to process even the simplest thoughts. My brain felt like it had shut down—not in panic, but in surrender. It was in that moment of stillness that I began to understand the toll of chronic stress and emotional depletion.

Burnout doesn't always announce itself with drama. Sometimes, it whispers through the absence of joy, the dullness of thought, and the quiet ache of disconnection. And sometimes, healing begins with a prayer, a pause, and the courage to admit you need rest.

Burnout doesn't always look like a breakdown. Sometimes it looks like going through the motions. Smiling when you don't mean it. Saying "I'm fine" when you're anything but. It sneaks in slowly, disguised as ambition, dedication, or resilience. But underneath, it's depletion. It's the cost of ignoring your limits.

The wake-up call came when I started forgetting things—simple things. I'd walk into a room and forget why. I'd reread the same sentence five times. I'd miss appointments I had scheduled myself. My brain, once sharp and reliable, felt like it was underwater. And emotionally, I was flat. I wasn't sad. I wasn't angry. I was just... blank.

That's when I knew I needed to reset.

The first thing I did was stop. Not forever. Not dramatically. Just enough to breathe. I took a few days off work. I turned off notifications. I let myself sleep. Not just rest—but deep, uninterrupted sleep. It felt indulgent at first, like I was letting people down. But the truth is, I had been letting myself down for years. And sleep was the first act of self-respect.

Sleep is not a luxury—it's a lifeline. It's where the brain repairs, the body heals, and the soul exhales. Studies show that chronic sleep deprivation impairs memory, emotional regulation, and decision-making (Walker, 2017). I didn't need science to tell me that—I felt it.

But knowing that sleep was part of recovery helped me give myself permission.

Next, I simplified. I looked at my calendar and asked, "What's essential?" Not what's expected. Not what's urgent. But what's truly necessary. I canceled meetings. I postponed projects. I said no. That was hard. I'm a helper by nature. Saying no felt selfish. But burnout had taught me that saying yes to everything was unsustainable. Boundaries weren't barriers—they were bridges back to health.

I also began reconnecting with my body. During burnout, I had treated my body like a machine—fuel it, push it, ignore it. But now, I listened. I stretched. I walked. I ate slowly. I drank water. I breathed. These small acts of care reminded me that I wasn't just a brain with deadlines—I was a whole person with needs.

One of the most healing moments came during a walk in the woods. I hadn't planned it. I just felt pulled to nature. The trees were quiet. The air was crisp. And for the first time in weeks, I felt present. Not productive. Not useful. Just present. That walk didn't solve everything. But it reminded me that healing doesn't always happen in big moments. Sometimes, it happens in the quiet ones.

I also began journaling—not to be profound, but to be honest. I wrote about my exhaustion, my fears, my guilt. I let the words spill out without editing. And in that mess, I found clarity. I saw patterns. I named pain. I reclaimed parts of myself I had buried under busyness.

Therapy helped too. Talking to someone who could hold space for my burnout without judgment was transformative. I learned that burnout isn't a failure—it's a signal. A signal that something needs to change. That I need to change. That my life needs to make room for me again.

Spiritually, I returned to stillness. I stopped trying to perform for God. I stopped trying to earn peace. I just sat with Him. I read Psalm 23 slowly, like a balm: *"He makes me lie down in green pastures. He leads me beside still waters. He restores my soul.*" That verse became my anchor. Not just poetic—but practical. I needed stillness. I needed restoration. I needed soul care.

I began practicing Sabbath—not as a religious tradition, but as a rhythm of rest. One day a week, I unplugged. I didn't work. I didn't strive. I just existed. I read. I napped. I laughed. I let joy return in small doses. And over time, those doses added up.

Burnout recovery isn't linear. There were days I felt better, then crashed again. Days I wanted to be productive, then realized I wasn't ready. But I learned to honour the process. To trust that healing takes time. To believe that I was worth the effort.

I also learned to ask for help. That was humbling. I had built my identity around being capable, dependable, strong. But burnout stripped that away. And in its place, I found something softer. More honest. More human.

Now, I live differently. I check in with myself. I protect my energy. I celebrate rest. I've learned that recovery isn't just about bouncing back—it's about building a life that doesn't require constant bouncing.

So if you're feeling burned out—mentally, emotionally, spiritually—start here. Stop. Breathe. Sleep. Simplify. Move gently. Speak honestly. Ask for help. Sit with God.

You don't have to earn your way back. You just have to return.

And your mind—tender, tired, resilient—is ready to heal.

THE BRAIN-BODY CONNECTION

MOVEMENT AS A MENTAL RESET

I used to think that moving around was only good for my health—something you did to lose weight, get stronger, or check off a box on your wellness to-do list. I'd drag myself to the gym, work out, and leave feeling tired but not mentally changed. I didn't realize that movement could be more until I hit a wall in my emotions, mind, and spirit. Something more profound. Something that helps.

My mind was like a tangled ball of yarn for a while—thoughts going around in circles, feelings all tied up, and no clear answers. I tried everything, from journaling to talking it out to praying, but nothing worked. I was stuck. Then, one day, I went for a walk.

It wasn't on purpose. I just had to leave the house. Leave Kathleen and the children behind, since we all go for walks most weekends or during the weekday when the weather is nice outside. I put on my shoes, went outside, and started to walk. No earphones. No place to go. It was just me, the pavement, and the sound of my feet. And something changed. With every step, my mind started to relax. I took deeper breaths. My shoulders fell. I didn't figure anything out on that walk, but I felt better. More stable. More like me.

That was when I realized that movement wasn't just physical—it was good for my mind.

This is true according to science. Movement causes the brain to release endorphins, dopamine, and serotonin—chemicals that affect mood, lower stress, and improve brain function (Ratey, 2008). It improves blood flow to the brain, helps memory, and even encourages neuroplasticity, which is the brain's ability to change and grow.

But movement does more than biology—it connects us to our bodies. And when we reconnect with our bodies, we come back to ourselves.

I made moving around a daily habit. Not hard workouts and going to the gym, but moving on purpose. Stretches in the morning. Walks in the afternoon. Dancing in the kitchen. Stretches on the living room floor. These times were like my reset buttons. Movement helped me when my mind was busy. Movement calmed my anxiety when it came on. When sadness lingered, moving around made it less strong.

One great experience I had was when I went hiking in the woods. I was having a hard time—sad about a loss, unsure of my path, emotionally raw. I didn't want to talk. I didn't want to think. I just wanted to move. So I went hiking. Forest bathing. The trail was quiet, the trees were tall, and the air was fresh. And as I climbed, something inside me started to change. My steps matched the rhythm of my breathing. My mind slowed down. My heart opened up. I hadn't solved my problems by the time I got to the top, but I had found peace.

Moving around also helped me feel happy again. I had lost touch with pleasure while I was burned out. It seemed like every little thing was a job. But when I started dancing again—just for fun and for me— I remembered what it was like to be alive. To laugh. To feel the music in my bones. That happiness was healing. It reminded me that getting better isn't just about resting; it's also about starting over.

I've seen this change happen to other people too. I encourage several of my clients who are depressed, to go for walks every morning. It's starts with only ten minutes and then increase the time gradually.

Some of these walks became holy. As some expressed, they would watch the sun rise, listen to the birds, and feel the air on their skin. And little by little, they felt better. They got their energy back. Their minds becomes clear.

A friend started doing tai chi because he was so anxious. The slow, deliberate movements helped him control his breathing, calm his nervous system, and feel more in control. It wasn't a cure, but it was a companion—a soft, daily reminder that recovery is possible.

You don't have to move a lot to get results. It doesn't have to be planned or have a goal. It just needs to be on purpose. A way to say, "*I am here.*" "*I hear you.*" "*I'm taking care of myself.*"

I try to do something small even on days when I don't feel like moving—a few stretches, a walk around the block, a song that gets me moving. I know that moving isn't just about changing my body; it's also about changing my mind. It's about going from stuck to flowing, from numb to feeling, and from chaos to calm.

"***He makes my feet like the feet of a deer; he causes me to stand on the heights***" is a verse from Psalm 18 that resonates with me. Movement as a way to rise. As strength. As grace. I feel like I'm flying when I move—not just in the body, but also in the mind.

I've learned that the brain and body work together. How we treat our bodies affects how we think, feel, and heal. Moving is a way to stay alive—a way to start over, reconnect, and remember who we are.

If your mind is heavy, your thoughts are jumbled, or your spirit is tired, try moving. Not to get away, but to come back. To yourself. To your breath. To your power.

Your body knows what to do. Your brain is paying attention. And now they're ready to heal.

It wasn't always clear to me how closely my mind and body were linked. For a long time, I thought of them as two different systems. I used my brain to think, solve problems, and worry. My body was for doing, carrying, and putting up with things. I drank coffee to get through stress, stayed up late to ignore tiredness, and tried to outsmart anxiety without ever moving. But eventually, my mind started to break down. I couldn't concentrate. I felt emotionally weak. And no amount of mental work could make it better.

Then one morning, I woke up feeling heavy—both in my body and in my mind. I didn't want to say anything. I didn't want to write. I didn't want to use my brain. I went outside and walked. No goal. No speed. Only movement. And something changed. The fog in my head started to clear with each step. I took a deeper breath. My mind became more gentle. I didn't feel "*better*," but I felt different. That difference was enough to keep me going.

That walk taught me something I hadn't learned in any book: moving is good for you—not just for the body, but also for the mind.

One afternoon, I was hit by a wave of anxiety I couldn't handle. My chest felt tight and my thoughts were racing. I couldn't stay still. So I got up, went outside, and started walking slowly. I paid attention to the sound of birds, the feel of the air, and the rhythm of my feet. My breathing returned to normal in a few minutes. My mind slowed down. I felt like I was back on solid ground.

That wasn't the only time that happened. Studies indicate that even short periods of physical activity can elevate mood, diminish anxiety, and augment cognitive performance (Mandolesi et al., 2018). You don't have to move a lot or for a long time for it to work. It just has to be consistent.

I also noticed that moving helped me deal with my feelings. Walking gave me space to feel when I was sad without drowning. Running helped me release anger without hurting anyone. Dancing made me feel alive when I was numb. Movement became a language that spoke when words couldn't.

Moving your body with awareness is a sacred thing. It's a way to pray, be present, and be kind to yourself. It says, "*I'm here.*" "*I'm paying attention.*" "*I'm responding.*" It brings us back to ourselves in a way that thinking alone can't.

I started to think of movement as a way to start over. I moved when my mind was full. I moved when I felt tired. I moved when I felt disconnected. Not to get away, but to come back.

One of the most surprising benefits was that movement helped me sleep better. I used to lie awake with my mind racing and my body tense. But on days when I moved—even a little—I fell asleep faster and slept better. That's not a coincidence. Physical activity helps regulate circadian rhythms and encourages the release of melatonin, the hormone that tells the body to sleep (Kredlow et al., 2015).

I also discovered that movement made me more creative. After a walk, ideas came more easily. After a stretch, problems seemed easier to solve. My brain felt more like a river than a pressure cooker. Movement didn't just make space—it made space.

Movement is now part of my daily routine. Not as a chore, but as a gift. A way to reset. To reconnect. To remember that I'm not just a mind trying to get by—I'm a body living it.

If your mind is racing, your heart is heavy, or your spirit is stuck, try moving. Not to change yourself, but to feel yourself. To change the energy. To unlock the window. To let something new in.

Your body is wise. Your brain is listening. And together, they're ready to heal.

THOUGHTS AND FEELINGS

ADJUST YOUR THINKING

I used to think that my thoughts were true—but they are not. If I thought it, it must be true. If I felt something, it must have been right. I didn't know my mind could lie to me. That it could distort, exaggerate, or repeat old stories that weren't helping me anymore. I didn't know I could change how I thought.

I started to question my thinking only when I was stuck—mentally, emotionally, and spiritually. It was a hard time. Everything felt heavy. I was second-guessing every choice I made and imagining the worst in every situation. I would wake up scared, go to bed worried, and spend the day trying to escape my own thoughts.

One afternoon, I was talking to Kathleen about how stressed I was. She listened patiently and then asked softly, *"What if the way you're thinking about this is making it harder?"* I stopped. That had never crossed my mind. I thought I was just reacting to what was happening. But maybe my thoughts were shaping it.

That question stuck with me. I started to see the patterns—how I made small problems seem big, how I assumed people were judging me, how I told myself I wasn't good enough. These thoughts weren't true; they were just habits. And habits can be changed.

I began practicing a different kind of awareness. I'd catch a thought and ask, *"Is this useful?"* Not *"Is this true?"*—because sometimes true thoughts that are based on facts aren't helpful. *"Is this helping me move forward or holding me back?"* That question changed everything.

I remember one morning when I was really anxious about a presentation I had to do. *"You're going to screw this up." "They'll see you don't belong." "You're not ready."* I felt stuck. But then I paused and asked, *"Is there another way to see this?"* I took a breath and said, *"You prepared. You care. It's okay to feel nervous."* The anxiety didn't disappear, but it softened. I could breathe again.

Changing the way you think doesn't mean pretending everything is okay. It means choosing a perspective that empowers you. It means turning fear into curiosity, harshness into kindness, and judgment into grace.

I began writing down the thoughts that bothered me and putting them on trial. I'd look for evidence. Then I'd write a counter-thought—not a denial, but a reframe. *"I can't take it anymore"* became *"I'm doing the best I can." "I failed"* became *"I learned something useful." "I can't move"* became *"I'm in transition."* These reframes didn't change my circumstances, but they changed how I felt about them.

One breakthrough came when I realized I didn't have to believe every thought that entered my mind. I could observe it, question it, and decide whether to keep it. That understanding set me free. It gave me back my agency.

I also started practicing gratitude—not to ignore pain, but to balance it. When my mind focused on what was missing, I gently brought it back to what was present: a warm cup of coffee, a kind note from a friend, a moment of peace. These small anchors helped me stay grounded.

Over time, changing my thoughts became a daily habit. Not a one-time fix, but a rhythm. I'd check in with myself. Notice my thinking. Where there was criticism, I offered kindness. Where there was fear, I offered hope. Where there was a lie, I offered truth.

I still have days when my thoughts spiral—when anxiety takes over, when old stories resurface. But now I know what to do. I know how to pause, reflect, and reset. I know how to speak to myself with the same compassion I offer others.

You are not your thoughts. You are the one who thinks. And you can choose a better lens.

Changing the way I thought wasn't just a mental exercise—it became a spiritual practice. God cares deeply about how we think. He knows that our thoughts shape our lives. Proverbs 23:7 says, "*For as he thinks in his heart, so is he*." Our thoughts are not neutral. They shape who we are, what we do, and how we relate to others.

I began paying attention to my inner dialogue. The way I spoke to myself. The beliefs I held. The fears I rehearsed. And I asked, "*Is this thought aligned with what God says?*" Often, the answer was no. I was believing lies about my worth, my future, and my ability to change. And those lies were keeping me stuck.

So I started replacing them—not with empty affirmations, but with Scripture. When I thought, "*I'm not enough*," I remembered 2 Corinthians 12:9: "*My grace is sufficient for you, for my power is made perfect in weakness.*" When I thought, "*I'll never change*," I held onto

Philippians 1:6: *"He who began a good work in you will carry it on to completion."* When I felt alone, I clung to Isaiah 41:10: *"Do not fear, for I am with you."*

These verses became anchors—not just words, but truths I could live by. They helped me shift from fear to faith, from shame to grace, from scarcity to abundance.

I also learned that renewing your mind is a daily practice. Paul says in Philippians 4:8, *"Whatever is true, whatever is noble, whatever is right, whatever is pure, whatever is lovely, whatever is admirable—if anything is excellent or praiseworthy—think about such things."* That verse became my filter. If a thought didn't fit, I didn't need to dwell on it.

Of course, it wasn't always easy. Some thoughts were loud. Some lies felt more familiar than truth. But I kept showing up. I kept replacing. I kept renewing. And slowly, my mind began to heal.

I remember one afternoon when I was stuck in indecision—paralyzed by overthinking. I went outside, sat in silence, and prayed. I asked God to help me see clearly. In that quiet moment, a verse came to mind: *"Trust in the Lord with all your heart and lean not on your own understanding"* (Proverbs 3:5). That was the shift I needed. I didn't have to figure it all out. I just had to trust.

Changing and challenging your thoughts doesn't mean ignoring reality. It means seeing it through the lens of God's truth. It means choosing faith over fear, hope over despair, and love over judgment.

Jesus modeled this beautifully. When He was tempted in the wilderness, He didn't argue—He responded with Scripture (Matthew 4:1–11). He showed us that truth wins the battle for the mind. And that truth is found in God's Word.

So when my thoughts start to spin, I pause. I breathe. I ask, *"What does God say about this?"* That question has changed everything.

If your mind feels heavy, your thoughts feel harsh, or your perspective feels stuck—start here. Change the way you think. Not with willpower, but with truth. Not with shame, but with grace. Not alone, but with God.

Your thoughts do not define you. You are the one who can give them new life. And your mind—beloved, strong, and capable of renewal—is ready to heal.

FIXED VS. GROWTH MINDSET

REFRAMING YOUR MENTAL LENS

I used to think that people either had talent or they didn't—that some were born with confidence, creativity, or intelligence, while others had to learn to live with their flaws. I didn't realize I had a fixed mindset. I thought I was being realistic, but I was really building walls around my own potential.

It showed up in small ways. I'd say things like, *"I'm not good at math,"* or *"I'm not creative."* I avoided challenges that made me feel vulnerable. I saw failure as proof that I wasn't good enough. When I saw others succeed, I assumed they had something I didn't—some secret ingredient.

I was working on a project that pushed me out of my comfort zone. It required me to speak in front of people in a new environment. I was asked to speak to police officers, social workers, nurses, doctors, mental health managers, and directors, which made me nervous. I was a bit shaky. I stuttered, forgot important points, and felt embarrassed—especially when speaking to a room full of professionals that are well educated. Part of me wanted to give up. I thought, *"I'm just not a good speaker for this group."* But my manager gently challenged me: *"What if you're just not a speaker yet to this group of people?"*

Those words—*yet*—broke something open inside me. Later that year, she arranged for me to speak to lawyers and judges from the Attorney General of Canada's office and invited me to present at monthly public meetings with managers from agencies supporting mental health.

I began learning about the concept of a growth mindset, developed by psychologist Carol Dweck. It's the idea that effort, learning, and persistence help people improve (Dweck, 2006). Failure isn't a sentence—it's feedback. Challenges aren't threats—they're opportunities.

I started changing how I spoke to myself. Instead of saying, *"I can't do this,"* I'd say, *"I'm learning how to do this."* Instead of *"I failed,"* I'd say, *"I found out what doesn't work."* These weren't just semantic shifts—they changed my perspective. And that changed my behaviour.

One of the interesting moments happened when I helped one of my daughters with her homework. She was frustrated, convinced she'd never understand fractions. I saw the same defeated look in her eyes that I used to have. I sat beside her and said, *"You don't have to get it right away. You just have to keep going."* We took our time, and when she solved a problem on her own, her whole face lit up. That moment reminded me that a growth mindset isn't just about achievement—it's about empowerment. Today she works as a manager in mental health.

I began applying this mindset to other areas of my life. I stopped labeling myself *"bad at communication"* when relationships were hard and started listening more. I stopped waiting for inspiration and began experimenting when I felt creatively stuck. I stopped asking, *"What's wrong with me?"* and started asking, *"What can I learn from this?"*

The change didn't happen overnight. I still had doubts. But now I had tools. I had hope.

I also realized how my fixed mindset had shaped my spiritual life. I'd think, *"I'll never be as faithful as him,"* or *"I'm not disciplined enough to pray consistently."* But Philippians 1:6 says, ***"He who began a good work in you will carry it on to completion."*** That means we're all in progress. God doesn't expect perfection—He invites participation. Every time we choose to learn, try again, or believe things can improve, we're aligning with His plan.

I've seen how this mindset shift has helped me in relationships, work, and faith. I've become stronger, more curious, and more compassionate. I've learned to praise effort, not just outcomes. To celebrate progress, not perfection. To look at myself and others with grace.

If you've ever felt stuck, discouraged, or defined by your limitations, know this: you can change your lens. You can shift from stagnation to growth. You can rewrite your story. You are not finished. You are a living work of art—learning, evolving, and expanding. And your mind is ready to grow because it is intelligent, adaptable, and full of potential.

I used to think the way I saw the world was the only way it could be—that my beliefs, reactions, and assumptions were fixed parts of who I was. I didn't realize I could change the lens I was looking through. That my mindset wasn't permanent—it was malleable. Something I could shape.

It took time to see that. I remember trying to work out at the gym. I was awkward, slow, and deeply uncomfortable. Every mistake felt like proof I wasn't good enough. I'd say things like, *"I'm just not wired for this,"* or *"I'm not one of those people can look fit and physically built."* And I believed it. I thought there was an invisible ceiling keeping me from reaching my potential.

Then I saw someone else—someone not naturally gifted—who kept showing up. They made mistakes. They struggled. But they didn't take failure personally. They didn't see it as judgment. They used it as fuel. And over time, they improved—not because they were born with it, but because they believed they could grow their muscles and gain the benefits of being at the gym. That guy became my trainer at the gym.

That's when I saw the difference between a fixed mindset and a growth mindset. A fixed mindset says, *"This is who I am."* A growth mindset says, *"This is who I'm becoming."*

I began noticing how often I used the fixed lens. Avoiding challenges to avoid looking foolish. Quitting early when progress felt slow. Comparing myself to others and feeling behind. These weren't just habits—they were beliefs. And they were holding me back.

I started experimenting with reframing. *"I'm not good at this"* became *"I'm not good at this yet."* When I felt discouraged, I'd ask, *"What is this teaching me?"* When I failed, I'd remind myself, *"This is part of the process."* These small shifts didn't erase the pain, but they changed how I carried it.

A major breakthrough came when I stopped believing that effort meant inadequacy. I used to think that if something was hard, it meant I wasn't meant to do it. Now I see effort as evidence of growth. Proof that I'm showing up. That I'm choosing change.

If you feel stuck, discouraged, or limited by your own limitations, you are not fixed. You are capable of change. You are growing.

And your mind is ready to grow. It's brave, flexible, and full of possibility.

COGNITIVE BIASES

HOW TO SPOT AND SHIFT THEM

I used to believe that I was a pretty reasonable person. I was proud of being fair, open-minded, and thoughtful. I thought I made choices based on facts and reason. But as time went on, I started to notice something odd: I kept getting caught in the same emotional traps. I would misjudge situations, assume the worst, or react in ways that didn't make sense—even to me. I couldn't see the blind spots in my brain.

That's when I first learned how our brains can trick us. It was both freeing and humbling. Humbling because I realized my mind wasn't as open as I thought. Freeing because I finally had words for the patterns that kept getting in my way.

Cognitive biases are mental shortcuts our brains use to quickly figure things out. They aren't really mistakes—they help us survive. But sometimes, they lead us astray.

These biases aren't character flaws; they're features of the human brain. We evolved to make quick decisions in uncertain situations, and those instincts still shape how we see the world today (Tversky & Kahneman, 1974). But in modern life, those shortcuts can distort our relationships, choices, and self-perception.

The first bias I noticed in myself was confirmation bias. I was doubting myself a lot and kept interpreting everything as proof that I wasn't good enough. If someone didn't respond to a message, I assumed they were upset with me. If I made a mistake, I saw it as evidence of failure. I was viewing the world through a lens of insecurity and only noticing things that confirmed it.

Confirmation bias is the tendency to seek, interpret, and remember information that supports what we already believe, while ignoring or dismissing evidence that contradicts it (Ruhl, 2023). It's powerful because it feels true. But once I recognized it, I started asking, *"What else could be true?"* Maybe that person was busy. Maybe mistakes are part of learning. Maybe I was doing better than I thought. That simple question didn't erase my doubt, but it created space.

Negativity bias is a frequent visitor. Our brains are wired to notice threats more than positive experiences—a survival instinct that helped our ancestors spot danger. But today, this bias can blind us to the good. After finishing a project, I'd fixate on one piece of critical feedback. I'd have a great day but obsess over one awkward moment. It was exhausting.

Negativity bias makes us focus more on negative events than positive ones, even when the positives are more significant (ScienceNewsToday, 2025). To counter it, I began practicing gratitude—not as a cliché, but as a balancing act. At the end of each day, I'd list three things that went well. Some days were hard. But even then, there was always something—a kind word, a laugh, a quiet breath. Over time, this habit reshaped my attention. I began to notice beauty more easily. I began to trust joy.

The fundamental attribution error was one of the hardest biases to confront. We tend to explain others' actions by their character and our own by circumstance. If someone cut me off in traffic, I'd think, *"What a jerk."* But if I did it, I'd think, *"I'm late and stressed."* This bias creates distance. It makes us judge instead of empathize.

I remember a time when a friend snapped at me unexpectedly. I was defensive. I thought, *"He's being rude."* But then I paused and asked, *"What might he be going through?"* It turned out he was grieving a loss I hadn't known about. That shift—from judgment to curiosity—changed everything. It softened my heart. It strengthened our bond.

Recognizing biases isn't about self-criticism. It's about awareness, compassion, and intentionality.

I've seen how cognitive biases affect relationships. The halo effect, for example, is when one positive trait makes us assume other positive traits. I once worked with someone who was incredibly charming. I assumed they were also trustworthy, kind, and honest. But over time, I realized that wasn't always true. They were human—flawed and complex. My bias had blurred the full picture.

One negative trait or moment can colour our entire perception of someone. I've done this too. A single awkward conversation changed how I felt about someone. But when I looked deeper, I often found warmth, wisdom, and depth I would've missed.

The availability heuristic is one of the most common biases I've seen in myself and others. We judge how likely something is based on how easily we can recall examples. Even though flying is safer than driving, we might fear it more if we hear about a plane crash. This bias can fuel anxiety. It can make rare events seem common and common events seem rare.

I used to worry excessively about worst-case scenarios. My mind clung to sad stories and assumed they'd happen to me. But then I started asking, *"Is this fear based on facts or feelings?"* I checked real data. I talked to people with different perspectives. I reminded myself that my brain was trying to protect me—but I could choose a calmer response.

The self-serving bias also showed up. It's the tendency to credit success to our own efforts and blame failure on external factors. When I succeeded, I'd think, *"I worked hard."* When I failed, I'd think, *"The system was unfair."* This bias can protect our self-esteem, but it can also block growth.

Now I ask, *"What part of this result was mine?"* Not to blame myself—but to take ownership. To learn. To evolve.

Hindsight bias is another subtle trap—the feeling that we *"knew it all along"* after something happens. I've said things like, *"I knew that relationship wouldn't last,"* or *"I had a feeling that project would fail."* But the truth is, I didn't know. I had guesses. Pretending I knew all along doesn't help—it just inflates my certainty.

Letting go of hindsight bias has made me more humble. More open. More helpful to others.

Anchoring bias is another quiet influencer. It's when we give too much weight to the first piece of information we receive. I've seen this in negotiations, first impressions, and decision-making. That first number, first thought, or first guess can shape everything that follows.

I remember shopping for a car and seeing a high price. Every other price I saw afterward was compared to that one—even when it didn't make sense. I had to step back and ask, *"What's the real value here?"* That question helped me make a better choice.

You don't have to be perfectly rational to recognize cognitive biases. That's not possible. We're human. We have emotions. We're shaped by stories and experiences. But when we notice our biases, we gain freedom. We see more clearly. We choose more wisely.

Curiosity is the best antidote to bias, in my experience. When I have a strong reaction, I ask, *"What's underneath this?"* When I make a snap judgment, I ask, *"What else could be true?"* When I feel stuck, I ask, *"Is this the only way to see it?"*

These questions don't always yield instant answers. But they open the door to better thinking. Kinder thinking. Expansive thinking.

I've also learned that community helps. Talking to people with different backgrounds, beliefs, and experiences has expanded my perspective. It's challenged my assumptions. It's reminded me that my view is one of many—and that truth often lives in the space between.

Faith has played a role too. Scripture reminds me that transformation begins in the mind. Philippians 4:8 offers a beautiful filter: *"**Think about things that are true, noble, right, pure, lovely, and admirable. If anything is excellent or praiseworthy—think about such things**."* That verse helps me shift from fear to faith, from judgment to grace, from bias to balance.

I still have blind spots. I still fall into traps. But now I know how to pause. How to reflect. How to reset.

If you've ever felt stuck in your thoughts, acted in ways that surprised you, judged yourself too harshly, or misunderstood someone else—you're not broken. You're human. And your brain—brilliant, imperfect, and capable of change—is ready to grow.

REFRAMING FAILURE

TURNING SETBACKS INTO LEARNING

When you fail, it can feel like everything is about you. There have been times when a setback didn't just feel like something that happened—it felt like something I was. I would take the disappointment and wear it like a badge, letting it change how I saw myself. It took me years to figure out that failing doesn't mean I'm a bad person. It shows how hard you worked, when you did it, and how much you've grown.

One of the most life-changing experiences I had was when I was in charge of the Social Worker Professional Practice at three hospitals and started a program to help people in the community. I was excited, ready, and eager to make a difference. But halfway through, things began to fall apart. Communication broke down. Deadlines were missed. People lost interest. I felt responsible. I was embarrassed. I thought, *"This isn't for me."*

After the project ended, I sat down with a manager who had seen it all unfold. She said, *"You didn't fail. You got smarter. You saw what works and what doesn't. You showed up. That means something."* Her words didn't erase the pain, but they changed the way the story was told. I began to see the experience as a classroom instead of a failure.

That's what reframing can do. It doesn't deny the pain—it gives it purpose.

Carol Dweck's work on mindset has been instrumental in helping people rethink failure. In her research, she distinguishes between a fixed mindset, which assumes abilities are static, and a growth mindset, which believes abilities can be developed through effort and learning (Dweck, 2006). People with a growth mindset are more likely to embrace challenges, persist through setbacks, and view failure as a natural part of growth.

I began adopting this mindset in small ways. I stopped saying, *"I'm a terrible cook,"* when I burned a meal. I said, *"I'm learning."* When I botched a presentation, I wouldn't say, *"I'm not a good speaker."* I would say, *"I'm getting better."* These weren't just changes in language—they were shifts in perspective. They helped me stay engaged, curious, and kind to myself.

One of the most powerful reframes I've embraced is seeing failure as proof that I tried. It means I took a risk and cared enough to act. That's not weakness—that's courage.

I've seen this in parenting too. A friend felt guilty after a rough patch with her teenage son. She thought she had let him down. But when she reflected, she saw the effort, the love, and the attempts to connect. She realized failure wasn't the absence of success—it was part of the journey toward trust. That insight helped her extend grace, and their relationship began to heal.

Reframing failure also means recognizing the context. Sometimes things fall apart due to timing, resources, or factors beyond our control. That doesn't mean we're not enough—it means we're human. Brené Brown says, "Failure is an imperfect ending, not a measure of your worth" (Brown, 2015). That truth has helped me release the need for perfection and embrace the freedom to be myself.

I've learned that storytelling is a powerful tool for reframing. When I share my failures—not as confessions but as lessons—I feel lighter. I feel connected. And often, others share their stories too, creating a shared space for growth.

I remember giving a speech at a workshop where I told a story about a business idea that didn't work out. Kathleen and I owned a household business at one time. I talked about the excitement, the missteps, and the disappointment. Someone came up to me afterward and said, "Thank you. I thought I was the only one." That moment reminded me that failure, when shared, can be a bridge—not a wall.

Changing our expectations is also part of reframing. We live in a culture that celebrates fast success, flawless outcomes, and highlight reels. But real growth is messy. It's nonlinear. It's full of detours. When we expect perfection, we invite shame. But when we expect progress, we make space for grace.

Now I ask myself, *"What does success look like today?"* Sometimes it's just showing up. Sometimes it's trying again. Sometimes it's taking a break. That question helps me honour the process instead of chasing an ideal.

Reframing my spirituality has been deeply healing. In the Bible, failure is never the end of the story. Moses doubted himself. Jonah ran away. David fell. Yet God used each of them in powerful ways. Their failures became turning points.

Isaiah 43:19 says, *"**See, I am doing a new thing!**"* That verse grounds me. *"**Now it springs up; do you not perceive it?**"* It reminds me that even when something ends, something new can begin. That failure can be fertile ground for growth.

I've also found comfort in 2 Corinthians 12:9: *"**My grace is sufficient for you, for my power is made perfect in weakness**."* That verse reframes weakness—not as a flaw, but as a doorway to God's strength. It reminds me that I don't have to be perfect to have purpose.

Reframing failure doesn't mean avoiding pain. It means honouring it—and then choosing a new story. It means asking, *"What did I learn?"* *"How did I grow?"* *"What will I do differently next time?"* These questions turn setbacks into stepping stones.

Failure has become part of my rhythm. When things don't go as planned, I take a walk. I breathe. I reflect. I write down three things I learned. Then I write down one thing I'm proud of—even if it's just trying. That ritual helps me move forward with intention.

And I've learned to celebrate others when they fail too. Not because they fell—but because they dared. Because they're growing. Because they're human.

I don't rush to fix things when a friend tells me they're upset. I pay attention. I agree. I say, *"Thanks for trusting me with this."* That answer makes things safe. It reminds us that failure isn't something to be ashamed of—it's something to embrace.

I've seen teams thrive in the workplace when failure is treated as normal. When leaders say, *"Let's talk about what didn't work,"* they create space for new ideas. It fosters a culture of learning rather than fear. One study found that companies that accept failure as part of learning are more flexible, creative, and resilient (Edmondson, 2011).

I've started using the phrase *"failing forward."* It means moving through failure with purpose. It means letting each failure shape what you do next. It means trusting that things are improving, even when you can't see it yet.

Looking back, I can see turning points in my biggest failures. Moments when I was stretched, refined, and redirected. I can trace the beginnings of wisdom, compassion, and strength.

If you're struggling—if something didn't go as planned, if you're unsure what to do next, or if you feel like you've failed—you're not alone. And you're not done. Failure isn't the end. It's the invitation to begin again, with more knowledge, courage, and heart. Your story is still unfolding. And your mind—strong, reflective, and ready—can grow.

I started failing early. I remember being terrified of getting the wrong answer in school. I'd rather stay silent than risk looking foolish. That fear followed me into adulthood. I avoided challenges that felt too big, too risky, or too uncertain. I told myself I was being wise, but really, I was shielding myself from the sting of failure.

Then came a moment that changed everything. I had poured months into a creative project I deeply believed in. I pitched it to a panel I admired, hoping they'd support it. But the response was lukewarm. The proposal was rejected. I felt crushed. I questioned my skills, my instincts, my worth. I nearly gave up.

But then I paused. I asked myself, "*What if this isn't the end*?" What if this is the beginning of something better? That question didn't erase the pain, but it shifted my perspective. I revisited the feedback—not as criticism, but as insight. I saw gaps I hadn't noticed. I refined my ideas. I tried again. The project was accepted the second time—and not just accepted, but celebrated.

That experience taught me that failure isn't a wall—it's a door. And it takes courage, curiosity, and compassion to walk through it.

Psychologists call this "reframing"—changing how we interpret something so we can see it in a more empowering light. It's a core principle of cognitive behavioral therapy and a powerful tool for emotional resilience (Beck, 2011). When we reframe failure, we move from shame to growth, from loss to discovery.

One of the most helpful shifts I've made is seeing failure as feedback. It's data. The world saying, *"Try a different way."* When I stopped treating setbacks as drama and started treating them as information, I became more creative, persistent, and open.

I've seen this in others too. A friend applied for his dream job and didn't get it. He was devastated. But instead of shutting down, he asked the hiring manager for feedback. That conversation led to mentorship, which led to a new job—one that fit him even better. His willingness to learn turned rejection into redirection.

Another friend launched a business that struggled in its first year. He felt embarrassed, especially when comparing himself to others. But he stepped back, analyzed what wasn't working, and pivoted. He refined his product, rethought his marketing, and built a loyal customer base. His business is thriving now—not in spite of failure, but because of it.

These stories remind me: failure isn't a detour on the road to success—it's part of the road.

Neuroscience backs this up. When we fail, the amygdala—our brain's emotional center—lights up, signaling distress. But the prefrontal cortex, responsible for planning and problem-solving, also activates. This dual response gives us a unique opportunity: if we engage our prefrontal cortex instead of staying stuck in emotion, we can grow (Bodiu, 2024).

Even more encouraging is the concept of neuroplasticity—the brain's ability to rewire itself in response to new experiences. When we learn from failure, we literally strengthen the neural pathways that support creativity and resilience (Doidge, 2007). Failure helps our brains grow.

But reframing failure isn't just cognitive—it's emotional. It requires self-compassion. It's easy to blame ourselves when we fall short. To say, *"I should've known better,"* or *"I'm not cut out for this."* But self-compassion says, *"This is hard, and I'm doing my best."* That gentler voice makes it easier to rise again. Research shows that people who treat themselves kindly after failure are more likely to persevere (Neff, 2011).

I speak to myself the way I'd speak to a friend. I don't pile on shame when I mess up. I ask, *"What can I learn from this?"* That question opens the door to growth.

I also started journaling after setbacks—not to vent, but to reflect. I'd write what happened, how I felt, and what I could do differently next time. That practice helped me process my emotions and extract meaning. It turned failure into fuel.

One of the most surprising shifts came during a season of personal loss. I made a decision I believed was right, but it broke my heart. I felt like I had failed—not just in action, but in judgment. I questioned everything. But over time, I saw that experience as a teacher. It clarified my values, boundaries, and the kind of love I want to build. It didn't feel like growth at first—but it was. Pain can be a profound instructor.

Faith has helped me reframe failure too. Scripture is full of stories where things go wrong—and people grow. Peter denied Jesus three times, yet became the rock of the early church. Paul persecuted Christians, then became one of their greatest advocates. These stories remind me that failure doesn't disqualify us—it prepares us.

Romans 5:3–4 says, ***"We rejoice in our sufferings, knowing that suffering produces endurance, and endurance produces character, and character produces hope."*** That verse has carried me through many dark nights. It reminds me that failure isn't the end—it's a beginning.

I also find comfort in Proverbs 24:16: *"**Though the righteous fall seven times, they rise again.**"* Reframing is about rising. It's the decision to see failure as a step, not a stop.

Now, when I face a setback, I pause. I breathe. I ask, *"What can I learn from this?"* That question doesn't erase the pain—but it gives it purpose.

I've learned to celebrate effort, not just outcomes. To value progress over perfection. To see myself and others through the lens of grace.

Reframing failure doesn't mean pretending it doesn't hurt. It means honoring the pain—and then moving forward. It means finding the lesson in the loss, and the wisdom in the wound.

So if you're struggling—if something didn't go as planned, if you're questioning your path, if you feel like you've failed—know this: you're not alone. And you're not finished.

Failure isn't the end. It's an invitation to begin again—with more wisdom, more courage, and more heart.

Your story is still unfolding. And your mind—strong, reflective, and ready—is growing.

NEUROFAITH

TRANSFORMED BY RENEWING THE MIND

One of the most powerful and life-changing things a person can do is renew their mind. This is true not only spiritually, but also biologically, emotionally, and behaviourally. Paul's words in Romans 12:2—"***Do not conform to the pattern of this world, but be transformed by the renewing of your mind***"—are more than poetic. He was describing a process that modern neuroscience now confirms: our brains can change, and so can we.

Neuroplasticity is the scientific foundation for this truth. It means the brain can rewire itself by forming new neural connections. What we think, feel, and do repeatedly shapes these pathways. If we dwell on fear, shame, or anger, those pathways strengthen. But when we meditate on truth, grace, and hope, we begin to build new pathways that lead to peace, clarity, and spiritual alignment. This isn't just theory—it's visible in brain scans and behavioral studies. Rewiring the brain is what it means to renew the mind.

I've experienced this firsthand. Years ago, I was deeply anxious. My thoughts constantly spiraled toward worst-case scenarios, self-doubt, and fear of failure, especially when working in psychiatry and one of the patient hang himself. I didn't realize it then, but I was rehearsing fear daily, reinforcing those neural pathways.

Change began when I intentionally meditated on Scripture—verses like Isaiah 26:3, "***You will keep in perfect peace those whose minds are steadfast, because they trust in you,***" and Philippians 4:6–7, "***Do not be anxious about anything…***"

I wrote them down, spoke them aloud, and visualized their truth. Over time, my mind began to shift. The anxiety didn't vanish overnight, but it weakened. I was experiencing neuroplasticity through spiritual renewal.

The Bible is full of stories where transformation begins with a change in thinking.

The woman with the issue of blood in Mark 5 had suffered for twelve years. She'd spent all she had on doctors, yet her condition worsened. But then something shifted—not in her body, but in her mind. "*She said to herself, 'If I just touch his clothes, I will be healed.'*" That thought, born of faith, was the catalyst. She believed, acted, and was healed. Her healing began in her mind.

In Luke 19, Zacchaeus—a wealthy but spiritually bankrupt tax collector—heard Jesus was coming. "*I have to see Him,*" he thought. That thought led him to climb a tree, an act of humility and desperation. When Jesus called him down and visited his home, Zacchaeus responded with generosity and repentance. His transformation began with a shift in perspective.

The woman at the well in John 4 arrived burdened by shame and isolation. But after her encounter with Jesus, she saw herself differently. She went from hiding to proclaiming: *"Come see a man who told me everything I ever did."* Her renewed mind led to boldness, and her testimony brought many to faith.

The prodigal son in Luke 15 hit rock bottom. *"He came to his senses,"* Scripture says. He thought, *"My father's servants have food to spare, and here I am starving."* That thought led him home, where he was embraced, restored, and celebrated. His return began with a renewed mind.

Moses in Exodus 3 doubted his calling: *"Who am I to go to Pharaoh?"* But God replied, ***"I will be with you."*** Moses had to shift from inadequacy to trust. That change empowered him to lead a nation to freedom.

Gideon in Judges 6 questioned his worth: *"How can I save Israel? My clan is the weakest."* But God called him a ***"mighty warrior."*** Gideon had to see himself through God's eyes. That shift led him to victory with just 300 men.

Esther hesitated when her people were threatened. But after Mordecai's encouragement, she declared, *"If I perish, I perish."* That mindset gave her courage, and her bravery saved a nation.

David, after his sin with Bathsheba, cried out in Psalm 51, ***"Create in me a clean heart, O God, and renew a steadfast spirit within me."*** He knew transformation began within. God restored him, and David continued to lead, worship, and write psalms that comfort generations.

Peter denied Jesus three times. But after the resurrection, Jesus restored him: ***"Do you love me?"*** Peter's renewed mind led him to preach at Pentecost, lead the early church, and write letters that still guide believers. His transformation became legacy.

Paul, who wrote Romans 12:2, experienced radical change on the road to Damascus. Once a persecutor of Christians, he became a passionate apostle. *"I press on toward the goal,"* he wrote in Philippians 3. His renewed mind fueled his mission, leading to church plants, letters, and a reshaped faith tradition.

These stories show that transformation begins in the mind. Before healing, action, or breakthrough—there's a thought. A shift. A moment of clarity. And that moment becomes the beginning of something new.

Neuroscience affirms this. When we think new thoughts—especially those rooted in truth and hope—we activate different brain regions. Repetition strengthens these pathways. Over time, our default thinking changes. We become less reactive, more reflective. Less anxious, more grounded. More aligned with God, less conformed to the world.

Science says the brain changes through repeated thought, emotion, and behaviour. Scripture says transformation begins with renewing the mind. Together, they declare a powerful truth: change is possible, and it starts within.

It's not a one-time event—it's a daily choice. To meditate on Scripture. To challenge lies. To replace fear with faith. To let God's Word reshape our thoughts, beliefs, and identity. As we do this, we live out Romans 12:2. We stop conforming to the world's patterns and start transforming through renewed minds.

Each of these biblical figures had a turning point—a moment when their thinking shifted. That shift led to action, which led to transformation. The renewed mind was the catalyst for healing, salvation, leadership, reconciliation, and purpose.

The process is simple but profound: thought → action → outcome. Romans 12:2 follows this pattern. We change when we renew our minds. And when we change, we begin to live out God's will—good, pleasing, and perfect.

These stories aren't just ancient—they're mirrors. They reflect our lives. They show that no matter where we begin—shame, fear, doubt, failure—a renewed mind can lead to healing, meaning, and joy. The results are real. And they begin with one true thought.

MENTAL AGILITY

TRAINING YOUR BRAIN TO PIVOT QUICKLY

I didn't always know how to pivot. In fact, for most of my life, I clung to plans like a lifeline. I liked knowing what was coming next. I liked structure, predictability, and the illusion of control. But life, as it tends to do, had other ideas.

One of the most defining moments came when I was laid off from a job I loved. It wasn't personal — just restructuring. But it felt personal. I had built my identity around that role. I had poured myself into it. And suddenly, it was gone. I remember sitting in my car afterward, staring at the steering wheel, feeling like the ground had shifted beneath me. I didn't know what to do next.

That was the first time I truly understood the need for mental agility. Not just the ability to think fast, but the ability to think differently. To shift gears. To adapt. To reimagine.

At first, I resisted. I tried to recreate what I had lost. I applied for similar roles, tried to replicate the same structure. But nothing fit. It was like trying to wear clothes that no longer matched my shape. Eventually, I realized I wasn't meant to go back — I was meant to move forward. But to do that, I had to pivot. And to pivot, I had to train my mind to let go.

Letting go is hard. It feels like surrender. Like failure. But mental agility reframes letting go as evolution. It's not about giving up — it's about growing up. It's about releasing what no longer serves so you can receive what's next.

I started small. I gave myself permission to explore. I took on psychotherapy and schooling. I learned new skills. I followed curiosity instead of certainty. I went into private practice and completed my second doctorate degree in Clinical Psychology. And slowly, my brain began to stretch. I became more comfortable with ambiguity. More open to possibility. More willing to change course.

I also began practicing scenario thinking. Instead of clinging to one outcome, I'd imagine multiple possibilities. What if this works? What if it doesn't? What's my next move either way? This helped me stay nimble. It reduced the fear of failure and increased my sense of agency.

One day, I was invited to speak at a conference — a new opportunity, but outside my comfort zone. My first instinct was to decline. I didn't feel ready. But then I remembered: agility isn't about being ready. It's about being willing. So I said yes. I prepared. I practiced. I showed up. And it went well — not perfectly, but authentically. That experience opened doors I hadn't even known existed.

Mental agility also means being able to shift emotional states. I used to get stuck in moods — frustration, sadness, anxiety. But I learned that emotions are data, not destiny. They're signals, not sentences. When I feel overwhelmed, I ask, "What's this emotion trying to tell me?" That question helps me pivot from reaction to reflection.

One of the most surprising lessons came from parenting. Children are naturally agile. They pivot constantly — from joy to tears, from play to rest, from one idea to the next. Watching them taught me that agility isn't chaos — it's creativity. It's responsiveness. It's life in motion.

I remember a day when one of my daughters spilled juice all over a project I was working on. My first reaction was frustration. But then I looked at her face — wide-eyed, apologetic, vulnerable. I took a breath. I pivoted. I said, "It's okay. Let's clean it up together." That moment became a memory — not of a ruined project, but of connection.

Mental agility also shows up in how we handle uncertainty. I used to crave answers. I wanted clarity before I could act. But now I understand that clarity often comes after action. That sometimes, you have to move before you know. That agility means trusting the process.

Faith has deepened this understanding. Proverbs 16:9 says, "*In their hearts humans plan their course, but the Lord establishes their steps*." That verse reminds me that agility isn't just mental — it's spiritual. It's about surrendering control while staying engaged. It's about listening for guidance and being willing to follow.

I've learned to pray differently. I don't just ask for outcomes — I ask for openness. For wisdom. For the ability to pivot with grace. That posture has changed everything.

In relationships, mental agility means being able to shift roles — from speaker to listener, from defender to empathizer, from fixer to companion. It means being able to say, "I was wrong," or "I see it differently now." It means choosing connection over being right.

I've had conversations where I started out rigid and ended up transformed — not because the other person changed, but because I did. Because I was willing to pivot. To soften. To grow.

In work, agility means being able to shift strategies. To respond to feedback. To innovate. I've seen teams thrive when they embrace agility — when they say, "Let's try it this way," or "What if we did something different?" That mindset creates momentum. It turns obstacles into opportunities.

One study from Harvard Business Review found that agile teams are more productive, more creative, and more resilient (Rigby et al., 2016). That's not just a corporate insight — it's a human one. Agility helps us thrive.

I've also learned that agility requires rest. You can't pivot well if you're depleted. You need margin. You need space. You need recovery. I've started building rest into my rhythm — not as a reward, but as a requirement. That rest fuels responsiveness.

Now, when I face change, I don't panic. I pause. I breathe. I ask, "What's the next right step?" That question helps me move forward with intention.

Mental agility isn't about being perfect. It's about being present. It's about responding instead of reacting. It's about choosing growth over rigidity.

If you're facing change — if life feels uncertain, if your plans are shifting, if your mind feels stuck — I want you to know: you can train your brain to pivot. You can build mental agility. You can move with wisdom, with courage, with heart. Your mind — flexible, curious, resilient — is ready to grow.

I used to think mental agility was something reserved for high-powered executives, emergency responders, or chess champions. People who had to make split-second decisions under pressure. It sounded like a skill you either had or didn't — like being double-jointed or ambidextrous. But over time, I realized that mental agility isn't just for crisis moments. It's for everyday life. And it's something we can all cultivate.

Mental agility is the ability to shift your thinking quickly and effectively in response to change, challenge, or uncertainty. It's the opposite of rigidity. It's what helps us adapt when plans fall apart, when conversations take unexpected turns, or when life throws curveballs we didn't see coming. And if I'm honest, I didn't start developing it until life gave me no other choice.

One of the most powerful shifts came when I stopped asking, "Why is this happening to me?" and started asking, "What is this teaching me?" That question didn't erase the discomfort, but it gave it purpose. It helped me move from victim to student. From resistance to resilience.

I remember a moment when I was preparing for a presentation that got canceled last-minute. I had spent days crafting it, rehearsing it, investing in it. When I got the news, I felt deflated. But instead of spiraling, I paused. I asked, "How can I use this material in a different way?" That question led to a blog post, which led to a podcast episode, which led to a conversation that opened a new door. The pivot didn't just salvage the effort — it expanded it.

Mental agility also means being able to hold multiple perspectives. I used to think in binaries — right or wrong, success or failure, good or bad. But life is rarely that simple. I began practicing "both/and" thinking. I could be disappointed and grateful. I could feel uncertain and hopeful. I could acknowledge loss and still look for growth.

This kind of thinking requires emotional flexibility. It means making space for complexity. For nuance. For contradiction. And that's not easy. Our brains crave clarity. But mental agility invites us to sit in the tension — to stay curious instead of rushing to conclusions.

Mental agility also shows up in how we handle feedback. I used to take criticism personally. I'd hear one negative comment and let it eclipse all the positive ones. But I've learned to separate feedback from identity. To ask, "What's useful here?" and "What can I learn?" That shift has made me more open, more teachable, more resilient.

One study from the University of Michigan found that people who practice cognitive flexibility — the ability to shift thinking and adapt to new information — are better at problem-solving, more emotionally balanced, and more successful in relationships (Scott et al., 2019). That makes sense to me. When we can pivot mentally, we can navigate life with more grace.

I've also seen how mental agility helps in conflict. When a conversation gets tense, it's easy to dig in, defend, or disengage. But agility invites us to listen differently. To ask questions. To explore instead of attack. I've had conversations where I started out feeling misunderstood, but ended up feeling connected — not because the facts changed, but because my posture did.

Mental agility isn't just about thinking fast. It's about thinking well. It's about slowing down when needed, speeding up when possible, and knowing which is which. It's about being able to shift gears — from analysis to intuition, from planning to improvising, from certainty to curiosity.

I've learned that agility grows through practice. It's like a muscle. The more we stretch it, the stronger it gets. I started doing small exercises — changing my routine, trying new things, asking different questions. I'd take a different route to work. I'd cook a new recipe. I'd read a book outside my usual genre. These small pivots trained my brain to be more adaptable.

One of the most surprising benefits has been creativity. When I stopped clinging to fixed ideas, I started seeing new possibilities. I'd combine concepts in fresh ways. I'd solve problems with more imagination. Mental agility opened up space for innovation.

I've also found that agility is contagious. When I model flexibility, others feel safer to do the same. In teams, in families, in friendships — agility creates room for collaboration. It helps us move together, not just individually.

I've learned to pray differently, too. Instead of asking for certainty, I ask for clarity. Instead of asking for control, I ask for courage. Instead of asking for answers, I ask for wisdom. That posture helps me pivot with peace.

Now, when life shifts — when plans change, when doors close, when surprises come — I try to respond with agility. I ask, "What's the invitation here?" That question helps me move forward, not just react.

I still have moments when I resist change. When I cling to comfort. When I feel stuck. But now I know how to breathe, reflect, and pivot. I know how to train my mind to move with grace.

If you're facing change — if life feels uncertain, if your plans are shifting, if your mind feels stuck — I want you to know: you can train your brain to pivot. You can build mental agility. You can move with wisdom, with courage, with heart.

Your mind — flexible, curious, resilient — is ready to grow.

FROM REACTIVE TO REFLECTIVE

SLOWING DOWN YOUR THOUGHT PROCESS

I used to pride myself on being quick. Quick to respond, quick to decide, quick to act. In conversations, I'd jump in with answers before the question was finished. In conflict, I'd defend myself before fully hearing the other person. In moments of stress, I'd rush to fix things — anything — just to feel in control. I thought speed was strength. But over time, I learned that speed without depth can be dangerous.

It wasn't until I found myself in a season of emotional exhaustion that I began to question my pace. I was reacting to everything — emails, texts, moods, news — like a pinball bouncing from one trigger to the next. My thoughts felt like a runaway train, and I was just a passenger. I wasn't choosing my responses. I was surviving them.

One day, after a particularly tense conversation with Kathleen my wife, I sat alone in my car and realized: I hadn't actually listened. I had defended, deflected, and decided — all within seconds. And now I was left with regret. That moment was a wake-up call. I didn't need to be faster. I needed to be slower. I needed to become more reflective.

Reflection isn't about overthinking. It's about intentional thinking. It's the pause between stimulus and response. It's the breath before the reaction. It's the space where wisdom lives.

I began practicing the pause. At first, it felt unnatural. I'd catch myself mid-reaction and say, *"Wait. Let me think."* Sometimes I'd excuse myself from a conversation just to breathe. Sometimes I'd write down my thoughts before responding. These small shifts created space — and in that space, I found clarity.

One of the first things I noticed was how often my reactions were rooted in fear. Fear of being misunderstood. Fear of losing control. Fear of being wrong. When I slowed down, I could name the fear. And once I named it, I could choose a different response.

I remember a moment at work when a colleague challenged one of my ideas. My instinct was to defend it — to prove my point, to protect my pride. But I paused. I asked myself, *"What's the goal here?"* The goal wasn't to win. It was to collaborate. So I listened. I asked questions. I considered their perspective. And together, we came up with something better than either of us could have done alone.

That experience taught me that reflection isn't weakness. It's wisdom. It's the ability to respond with intention instead of impulse.

Psychologists call this *"response flexibility"* — the capacity to pause, reflect, and choose a response that aligns with your values and goals (Siegel, 2007). It's a key component of emotional intelligence and a predictor of healthy relationships, effective leadership, and personal growth.

I started building reflection into my daily rhythm. In the mornings, I pray for ten to twenty minutes — not to be profound, but to be honest. I'd write down what I was feeling, what I was thinking, what I needed. That practice helped me start the day with clarity instead of chaos.

In conversations, I began listening more deeply. Not just to words, but to tone, emotion, and intention. I'd ask myself, "What's really being said here?" That question helped me move beyond surface reactions and into deeper understanding.

I also began practicing *"slow thinking"* — a concept popularized by Nobel laureate Daniel Kahneman. He describes two systems of thought: fast and intuitive (System 1), and slow and deliberate (System 2). While fast thinking is useful for routine decisions, slow thinking is essential for complex, emotional, or high-stakes situations (Kahneman, 2011).

I realized that many of my regrets came from fast thinking in moments that required slow thinking. So I started asking myself, "Is this a System 1 moment or a System 2 moment?" That question helped me shift gears.

One of the most transformative shifts came in my relationship with myself. I used to react to my own emotions with judgment. If I felt anxious, I'd criticize myself. If I felt sad, I'd try to snap out of it. But reflection taught me to respond with compassion. To say, "This is hard, and I'm doing my best." That kindness changed everything.

I remember the nights when I couldn't sleep, especially when the children were teenagers and would be out at night. Although they were respectful of their curfews, my mind used to think of the worst-case scenario. I was working with the police at that time and was exposed to traumatic cases with teenagers. My mind would be racing with worries. Instead of trying to silence them, I would get up, light a candle, and write my worries down. I asked myself, *"What's within my control? What's not? What do I need right now?"* That reflection didn't solve everything, but it soothed me. It reminded me that I could be gentle with my mind.

Reflection also helped me navigate grief. After losing someone I loved, my emotions were raw and unpredictable. I'd feel fine one moment and shattered the next. I used to react by pushing through, staying busy, avoiding the pain. But reflection invited me to sit with it. To ask, *"What is this sadness teaching me?"* That question opened the door to healing. It took me over twenty-six years to put closure to the death my of friend. I had to face reality and wished I had don't it sooner.

I've learned that reflection isn't just a skill — it's a sanctuary. It's where we meet ourselves. Where we make sense of our stories. Where we choose our path.

Faith has deepened this practice for me. Scripture is full of invitations to reflect. Psalm 46:10 says, *"**Be still, and know that I am God.**"* That verse reminds me that stillness isn't passive — it's powerful. It's where we hear the whisper beneath the noise.

Jesus modeled reflection when He would often withdrew to quiet places to pray, to think, to be. Before major decisions, after intense moments, in times of sorrow — He paused. He reflected. He listened. That rhythm inspires me.

One of the first verses that challenged my reactive nature was James 1:19: *"**Everyone should be quick to listen, slow to speak and slow to become angry.**"* That verse felt like a mirror. I was often slow to listen, quick to speak, and even quicker to anger — especially when I felt threatened or misunderstood. But James wasn't just offering advice. He was describing a posture of the heart. A way of being that reflects the character of Christ.

I began to practice this verse in real time. When someone said something that triggered me, I'd pause. I'd breathe. I'd silently pray, *"Lord, help me listen."* That pause — even just a few seconds —

changed everything. It gave me space to hear not just the words, but the heart behind them. It helped me respond with empathy instead of defensiveness.

Throughout the Gospels, we see Jesus responding to people with calm, clarity, and compassion. When the Pharisees tried to trap Him with questions, He didn't react — He reflected. He asked questions in return. He told stories. He paused. Even in moments of intense pressure, Jesus never rushed. He moved with purpose, not panic.

One of my favourite examples is in John 8, when the religious leaders bring a woman caught in adultery before Jesus. They demand a reaction. They want Him to condemn her. But instead of speaking immediately, Jesus bends down and writes in the sand. He pauses. He reflects. And then He responds with one of the most powerful statements in Scripture: *"Let any one of you who is without sin be the first to throw a stone at her."* (John 8:7)

That moment teaches us that reflection creates room for mercy. For truth. For transformation.

I've learned that slowing down isn't weakness — it's wisdom. Proverbs 14:29 says, *"Whoever is patient has great understanding, but one who is quick-tempered displays folly."* That verse reminds me that patience isn't passive. It's discerning. It's the ability to wait for clarity before acting.

I've asked God to show me what I couldn't see. And He did. He revealed my pride, my assumptions, my blind spots.

Reflection also helps us navigate temptation. In moments of weakness, our impulses can lead us astray. But Scripture invites us to pause, to consider the consequences, to seek God's wisdom. Proverbs 3:5–6 says, *"Trust in the Lord with all your heart and lean not on your own understanding; in all your ways submit to him, and he will make your paths straight."* That verse reminds me that my understanding is limited. That I need divine perspective. And that reflection is how I access it.

Ecclesiastes 3:1 says, *"There is a time for everything, and a season for every activity under the heavens."* That verse reminded me that sorrow has its place. That reflection isn't just for joy — it's for mourning. And in that space, I found healing.

Reflection also helps us grow in wisdom. Proverbs 2:2–6 encourages us to *"turn your ear to wisdom and apply your heart to understanding."* That doesn't happen in haste. It happens in stillness. In study. In prayer. In reflection.

I've learned to ask God for a reflective spirit. To help me slow down when I want to rush. To help me listen when I want to speak. To help me understand when I want to react. That prayer has changed the way I move through the world.

I've started incorporating spiritual reflection into my day. I read a verse, sit in silence, and ask, "What is God saying to me here?" That practice grounds me. It helps me respond with faith instead of fear.

In relationships, reflection has helped me become more present. I used to listen with half my attention — the other half planning my response. But now I try to listen fully. To reflect before I reply. To ask, *"What does this person need right now?"* That shift has deepened my connections.

I've also learned to reflect after conflict. Instead of replaying the argument, I ask, "What was I feeling? What was I protecting? What could I do differently next time?" That reflection turns tension into transformation.

In leadership, reflection has become a cornerstone. I used to think leaders had to have quick answers. But I've learned that the best leaders ask thoughtful questions. They pause. They consider. They reflect. That posture creates trust.

One study found that leaders who engage in regular reflection are more effective, more empathetic, and more innovative (Di Stefano et al., 2014). That makes sense to me. Reflection creates space for insight.

I've started ending each week with a reflection ritual. I ask myself three questions: What went well? What was hard? What did I learn? That practice helps me grow with intention.

I've also learned that reflection requires humility. It means admitting when we're wrong. When we've hurt someone. When we need to change. That honesty is hard — but it's holy.

Reflection also helps us navigate transitions. When life shifts — a move, a job change, a new season — it's easy to react with fear. But reflection invites us to ask, *"What is this transition asking of me?"* That question helps us move with grace.

I've learned that reflection isn't just for quiet moments. It's for busy ones too. It's the breath before the meeting. The pause before the reply. The silence before the decision.

Now, when I feel triggered, I try to pause. I ask, *"What am I feeling? What am I assuming? What do I want to choose?"* That pause is powerful. It helps me respond with wisdom.

Mental agility and reflection go hand in hand. Agility helps us pivot. Reflection helps us pivot well. Together, they create resilience.

If your reactions are costing you peace — if your thoughts are racing, if your emotions are loud, if your responses feel automatic — I want you to know: you can slow down. You can reflect. You can choose.

God isn't in a hurry. And He invites you to move at the pace of grace.

Your mind — thoughtful, tender, teachable — is ready to grow.

UNLEARNING

WHY LETTING GO IS JUST AS IMPORTANT AS LEARNING

I used to think that growth was all about getting more. More information. More skills. More understanding. I thought that new ideas, new habits, and new strategies would help me move forward. Learning has changed me in many ways, but I've learned that some of the most important changes in my life didn't come from adding something new— they came from letting something go.

Unlearning is a quiet revolution of the soul. It's the process of letting go of old beliefs, assumptions we've inherited, and automatic reactions that don't help us anymore. It's not forgetting—it's taking another look. It's letting go of what we used to think was true so we can make room for what is really true.

I first learned about the power of unlearning during a time of change in my life. I had just left a job that had defined me for a long time. I thought I knew myself—what I believed, what I wanted, and what I was good at. But without the title, the routine, and the familiar structure, I didn't know what to do. I kept trying to use old ways of thinking to deal with new situations, but nothing worked. I was trying to move forward while dragging the past with me.

One morning, while writing a new book, I wrote down the question, *"What do I need to unlearn?"* The answers came slowly, like whispers. I had to stop thinking that my worth was based on how much I did. I had to stop saying yes to everything. I had to stop being afraid of letting people down. That list became my guide—not to learn something new, but to let go of what was no longer true.

It's hard to forget what you know. It forces you to face what you've believed. To question what feels comfortable. To admit that you might have been wrong—or at least, not entirely right. It makes you feel small. But it's also freeing.

One of the first things I had to stop believing was that being vulnerable was a sign of weakness. I was raised in a place where being strong meant being stoic. Feelings were private. People hid their struggles. I learned to smile through pain, push through tiredness, and act like everything was fine. But that armor became a prison. I wasn't fully myself, so I couldn't connect deeply with others.

I didn't really connect with people until I started sharing my truth— the messy, imperfect, and tender parts. I remember telling a friend about a time when I was depressed after losing a close friend in Croatia while we were missionaries. I thought I would be judged. Instead, I was met with kindness. That moment taught me that being open and honest is brave, not weak. And I had to unlearn the lie that said otherwise.

I used to think that growth meant getting more things—gathering knowledge, skills, and experiences. I thought the more I learned, the more I would become. And for a time, that worked. I read the books, took the classes, and followed the advice. I learned how to get things done, how to talk to people, and how to be a leader. But eventually, I started to feel heavy—not with wisdom, but with noise. I was carrying too much. Too many assumptions, expectations, and beliefs that no longer fit the person I was becoming. That's when I realized that learning is only half the journey. The other half is unlearning.

Unlearning is the quiet work of change. It doesn't stand out. It doesn't come with awards or applause. But it's essential. It means letting go of old beliefs, habits we've learned from others, and stories we've internalized that no longer serve us. It's not forgetting—it's taking a second look. It's releasing what we thought was true so we can make room for what truly is.

I remember the first time I made a conscious effort to unlearn something. I was burned out, still trying to use the same strategies that had always worked for me: work harder, say yes, keep going. I was juggling three jobs, but those strategies weren't working anymore. I was tired, disconnected, and unsure who I was apart from my accomplishments. After working two shifts in a row one morning, I asked myself, *"What do I need to unlearn?"*

The answers came slowly. I had to stop believing that my worth was based on productivity. I had to stop overcommitting. I had to stop being afraid of letting people down. That list became my guide—not for learning something new, but for letting go of what was no longer true.

It's hard to unlearn what we didn't choose—the things we inherited from our parents, our culture, and our past. In the culture I grew up in, silence was strength. Vulnerability was weakness. Feelings were private. People hid their pain. I learned to smile through struggle and pretend everything was fine. But that armor turned into a prison. I couldn't connect with others because I wasn't showing up as myself.

I didn't start connecting until I began sharing my truth—the messy, flawed, and sensitive parts. I remember telling a friend about a time when I was deeply sad. I expected judgment but received kindness instead. That moment taught me that honesty is not weakness; it's strength. I had to unlearn the lie that said otherwise.

Another powerful unlearning happened in my spiritual life. For a long time, I thought I had to earn God's love. I believed that if I prayed enough, served enough, and sacrificed enough, I would finally be good enough. That belief made my faith heavy and fearful. I was always striving and never resting.

Then I encountered grace—not as an idea, but as a living truth. I read Romans 8:38–39: *"For I am sure that neither death nor life... nor anything else in all creation will be able to separate us from the love of God that is in Christ Jesus our Lord."* That verse undid me. It told me to stop believing in a performance-based faith and start believing in unconditional love.

Unlearning also happens in relationships. I used to think conflict was bad and meant something was wrong. So I avoided it. I did everything I could to keep the peace. But that avoidance only created distance. I wasn't being honest. I had to unlearn the idea that conflict is bad and learn that healthy conflict is necessary. It's how we grow, clarify, and build trust.

I remember having a hard conversation with a close friend about an issue that had lingered between us. It wasn't easy—but it helped. We came out with more respect, understanding, and connection. That experience taught me that letting go of avoidance can bring people closer together.

Unlearning has also shaped my work life. I used to think being an expert meant knowing everything, and that leadership meant certainty. But I've learned that the best leaders ask questions, listen, adapt, and change.

A study in the *Harvard Business Review* found that organizations that prioritize unlearning—deliberately discarding outdated practices—are more innovative, resilient, and successful (Bonchek & France, 2016). I understand that now. When we cling to what worked yesterday, we can't see what's possible today.

Unlearning also means letting go of identities that no longer fit. I used to define myself by my success. I felt lost when I wasn't achieving. But that mindset led to burnout. I had to unlearn the belief that my value depended on what I did. Even when I rest, I am still loved, worthy, and enough. It didn't happen overnight—it took prayer, therapy, and reflection. But over time, I began to feel more grounded. More whole. More free.

I've also had to unlearn cultural stories about success, beauty, and worth. I used to think success meant constant upward motion, beauty meant fitting into a narrow mold, and value meant comparison. But those beliefs drained me. They made me chase instead of live.

Now, I see success as alignment with purpose. Beauty as authenticity. Value as inherent. That shift has brought peace.

Unlearning is especially important during times of transition. When we move, lose someone, or start something new, our old ways of thinking might not work anymore. We have to release what doesn't fit to make room for what's next.

Faith invites us into this journey. Ephesians 4:22–24 says, *"You were taught... to put off your old self... and to be made new in the way you think."* That's what unlearning is about—shedding the old, welcoming the new, and embracing transformation.

Jesus often called people to unlearn. He said, *"You have heard it said... but I say to you..."* (Matthew 5). He invited people to let go of legalism and embrace love, to stop judging and start showing mercy, to move from religion to relationship.

Jesus was the master of unlearning. He challenged assumptions, broke barriers, and redefined truth. Faith isn't just about learning new things—it's about letting go of false ones.

The invitation still stands.

There are many calls in the Bible to unlearn. Ephesians 4:22–24 reminds us to *"put off your old self"* and *"be made new."* Philippians 3:13–14 says, *"I press on toward the goal,"* which means forgetting what's behind and reaching forward. Isaiah 43:18–19 says, *"Forget the former things; do not dwell on the past. See, I am doing a new thing."* These verses remind us that God is always doing something new—but we must first let go of the old.

I know it takes grace to unlearn. We won't always get it right. We'll slip back into old patterns. But every time we choose to let go, we grow.

I often ask myself, *"What am I holding onto that no longer serves me?"* That question keeps me open. It keeps me honest. It helps me stay free.

Unlearning doesn't mean erasing the past—it means seeing it differently. It's honoring what shaped us while choosing what will shape us next.

If you're feeling stuck—if something isn't working, if a belief feels heavy, or a habit feels hollow—it's okay to let go. It's okay to unlearn. You can change.

You are not who you were. You are not your habits. You are not your programming. You are a soul—alive, learning, and becoming.

And your mind, brave, curious, and strong, is ready to grow.

CURIOSITY OVER JUDGMENT

A New Approach to Problem-Solving

I used to think that finding the quickest answer was the best way to solve a problem. The goal was to fix, solve, and make things right as soon as possible. I thought of problems as puzzles to solve, not conversations to have. And when things didn't go as planned, I often fell back on judgment. I was hardest on myself, judging the situation and the people involved. I thought that being sure meant being right.

But as time went on, I learned that judging people closes doors. Curiosity lets them in.

The change didn't happen all at once. It came slowly, through times of stress, confusion, and failure. There was one day at work I remember when a project I was in charge of hit a wall. People missed deadlines, couldn't talk to each other, and were very angry. I wanted to find something wrong. Who messed up? What went wrong? Why didn't anyone say something sooner? I was ready to point fingers, take charge, and clean up the mess. But something inside me stopped. After taking a breath, I asked a different question: *What's going on here?*

That question made everything different. I stopped reacting and started listening instead. I asked my team how they were doing, what problems they were having, and what help they needed. And what I heard shocked me. People weren't lazy or careless—they were scared, confused, and too busy to speak up. I couldn't see the truth because of my judgment. But my curiosity helped me see it.

That experience taught me that being curious isn't a passive thing. It's strong. It's the desire to ask, to look into things, and to stay open. It's the decision to lean in rather than shut down. And when we look at problems with curiosity, we don't just fix them—we change them.

I started being curious in everyday situations. Instead of thinking the person who cut me off in traffic was rude, I thought they might be rushing to an emergency. Instead of feeling rejected when a friend didn't call me back, I thought they might be going through something. Instead of being hard on myself when I made a mistake, I asked what I could learn from it. These little changes made me feel better. They taught me to be more patient, kind, and open. It's like doing cognitive behavioral therapy on myself.

In relationships, curiosity is powerful. I used to think that agreeing with someone meant understanding them. But curiosity taught me that understanding is more about being present than trying to convince someone. It's about asking questions and not needing to control the answers.

I remember talking to a family member who had a very different view of the world than I did. We used to get into fights when we talked. But this time, I chose to be curious. I asked, *"Can you help me understand what you mean by this?*" And then I paid attention—not to argue, but to learn. That talk didn't change what we thought, but it did change how we felt about each other. We felt heard. We felt respected. We felt safe.

Being curious also helps us deal with uncertainty. Judgment makes us rush to decisions when we're scared or unsure. But curiosity makes us want to learn more—to get information, to stay with the unknown. I used to dislike uncertainty. I wanted clear answers, clear paths, and clear results. But life isn't always easy to understand. Being curious has helped me stay grounded in the fog.

A personal crisis was one of the most important moments in my life. I had to make a choice that seemed impossible. Each path carried risks, and there was no clear way forward. I wanted someone to tell me what to do. But instead, a manager asked me, *"What questions haven't you asked yet?"* That question broke something open inside me.

I realized I was so focused on finding the right answer that I hadn't looked at the problem from all angles. I started writing, praying, and thinking—not to find answers, but to gain understanding. Slowly, things became clearer. Not like a lightning bolt, but like a quiet opening.

Being curious is also a spiritual practice. Jesus asks more questions than He answers in the Bible. **"Who do you think I am?" "Do you want to get better?"** "What's making you scared?" These questions weren't for show—they were about relationship. They made people think, connect, and change. Jesus didn't hurry to heal people; instead, He invited them to look inside themselves.

I didn't realize how often I made snap judgments until I started slowing down and looking at my thoughts through the lens of the Bible. I always thought of myself as smart, thoughtful, and fair. But when I looked closer, I saw how quickly I came to conclusions—how often I thought I knew what people were up to, how easily I labelled things as good or bad, right or wrong—without ever asking God what He saw.

Quick judgment reacts. Fear often drives it—fear of being wrong, fear of getting hurt, or fear of losing control. But curiosity takes time. It's about relationship. It comes from love. And the more I learned about Jesus's life, the more I saw that He chose curiosity instead of judgment.

One of the most powerful examples is in John 4, when Jesus meets the Samaritan woman at the well. He could have judged her—she was a woman, a Samaritan, and someone who had lived a complicated life. But instead of judging her, Jesus asked questions. He asked about her life, her relationships, and her thirst—not just for water, but for truth. He didn't rush to help her; He invited her to talk. And that conversation led to transformation.

That story taught me that curiosity is a kind of grace. It says, *"I see you. I want to know you. I'm not here to shame you; I'm here to walk with you."* And when we act like that toward others, we make room for healing.

I've also seen how curiosity can help us grow spiritually. In Luke 10, a teacher of the law asks Jesus, ***"What do I have to do to inherit eternal life?"*** Jesus doesn't give a direct answer. Instead, He asks, *"What does the Law say? How do you read it?"* He invites the man to think, to look deeper, to engage. That moment reminds me that God doesn't just want us to remember the truth—He wants us to wrestle with it. To ask, to seek, to knock.

The Bible is full of curiosity. Proverbs 25:2 says, ***"It is the glory of God to conceal a matter; to search out a matter is the glory of kings."*** That verse reminds me that seeking is sacred—that asking questions is part of how God made us. God delights when we try to understand.

I used to think faith meant knowing everything. But now I understand that faith often starts with a question: *"Where are You, Lord?" "What's going on?" "What do You want me to know?"* These questions don't show doubt—they show relationship. They mean we're not just accepting doctrine, but engaging with God.

There are so many questions in the Psalms. David asks, *"How long, O Lord?" "Why are You hiding Your face?" "What is man that You are mindful of him*?" These aren't rhetorical—they're raw and real. God doesn't tell David to stop asking; He meets him right where he is.

Curiosity also helps us approach conflict with humility. Jesus says in Matthew 7, *"Do not judge, or you too will be judged."* Then He asks, *"Why do you look at the speck in your brother's eye and pay no attention to the plank in your own?"* That used to make me feel guilty, but now I see it as an invitation to be curious—to look inward and ask, *"What am I missing? What am I putting out there? What do I need to release?"*

There have been times when I was sure someone had wronged me. I built my case, practiced my arguments, and prepared to defend myself. But when I stopped and prayed, I heard a soft voice say, *"Ask them."* And when I did, I discovered something else—they weren't trying to hurt anyone; they were hurting. They weren't careless; they were overwhelmed. My judgment built a wall. Curiosity built a bridge.

Curiosity also helps us face failure with grace. Jesus doesn't shame Peter after he denies Him three times in John 21. He doesn't say, *"I told you so."* He simply asks, *"Do you love Me?"*—three times, once for each denial. Those questions weren't about blame; they were about restoration. Jesus was inviting Peter to reconnect, recommit, and remember who he was. That reminds me that God's questions are always meant to heal.

When I fail, I've learned to ask myself reflective questions: *"What was I feeling?" "What was I afraid of?" "What can I learn from this?"* Those questions help me move from judgment to grace.

Curiosity also deepens how I read Scripture. I used to read the Bible for answers. Now, I read it for conversation. I ask, *"What does this reveal about God's heart?" "What is the Spirit showing me?" "What am I being invited to notice?"* This posture has brought Scripture to life—it's no longer just a book; it's a dialogue.

The Bereans are called *"more noble"* in Acts 17 because they eagerly received the message and examined the Scriptures daily to see if what Paul said was true. That tells me that curiosity is holy—that God welcomes our testing, exploring, and questioning.

Curiosity also helps us love our neighbours well. When Jesus tells the story of the Good Samaritan in Luke 10, He's answering the question, *"Who is my neighbour?"* That question isn't just about geography—it's about empathy. Jesus responds with a story that challenges assumptions, breaks down barriers, and stirs compassion. It reminds me that curiosity leads to kindness.

I've started asking people more intentional questions: *"What's been on your mind lately?"* *"What's something you wish people knew about you?"* *"How can I support you right now?"* Those questions open doors that advice never could.

You also need curiosity in prayer. I used to come to God with a list. Now, I come with wonder. *"What are You doing in this situation?"* *"What do You want to show me today?"* *"What am I missing?"* Those prayers have brought new insights, gentle corrections, and unexpected peace.

God says in Isaiah 55, ***"My thoughts are not your thoughts, and your ways are not My ways."*** That reminds me I'll never fully understand God—but I'm invited to seek Him, to ask, to explore, to stay curious.

I've also started praying with more openness. I don't just ask God to fix things anymore; I ask Him to reveal what I'm missing. *"What am I avoiding?"* *"What am I afraid to feel?"* *"What am I resisting?"* Those prayers have brought deeper healing than any quick fix ever could.

Curiosity also helps us unlearn what we thought we knew. Many of our current beliefs were formed in childhood, shaped by culture, and reinforced by experience. But not all of them are true. I used to think asking for help was a sign of weakness—that I had to handle everything on my own. Curiosity made me question that. *Where did that belief come from? What has it cost me? What could change if I let it go?* That journey showed me a new truth: asking for help is strength. It honors our humanity.

I also had to let go of the belief that I needed to know everything. Curiosity showed me that wisdom isn't about certainty—it's about openness. It's about being willing to learn, to grow, and to change. That mindset has made me a better friend, leader, and person.

People who are curious inspire curiosity in others. I've seen this as a parent, teacher, and mentor. When we meet mistakes with curiosity instead of judgment, we create space for growth. I remember working with a child and youth worker at a hospital's Child and Adolescent Mental Health Unit who made a big mistake. She was terrified of being reprimanded. Instead of getting angry, I asked gently, *"What do you think happened here?"* She was honest, took responsibility, and learned from it. Even though she lost her job, she left more confident, not more afraid.

Curiosity also helps us face change. When life shifts—a move, a loss, a new season—it's easy to judge it: *"This is bad." "This isn't fair."* But curiosity invites a different question: *"What can I learn from this?"* That question doesn't erase pain, but it gives it purpose.

I've learned that curiosity is a form of love. It says, *"I care enough to ask. I care enough to listen. I care enough to stay."* That kind of love is revolutionary in a world that moves too fast.

If you're struggling in your work, your relationships, or your heart, I invite you to pause. Take a breath. Ask, *"What else could be true?"*

You might not get an answer right away, but it will point you toward one—toward a path, a possibility, a way through.

You don't have to know everything. You just need to stay curious.

Your mind is ready to grow because it is open, tender, and wise. And your heart is ready to hear from God because it is humble, seeking, and faithful.

THINKING IN SYSTEMS

MOVING BEYOND LINEAR THOUGHT

I used to think in straight lines for most of my life, very black and white thinking, until the children became teenagers and realized I needed to tap into grace. I used to think if A happened, then B would happen next. If I put in the effort, I would succeed. People would treat me well if I was nice. Things would go as planned if I made a plan and stuck to it.

This idea of knowing what would happen next was comforting. It made me feel like I was in charge.

But life doesn't always go in straight lines. It goes in circles. It crosses. It surprises.

Everything changed when I started to look at the world through systems, and I owe it to parenting seven children and over 35 years of marriage as of August 11, 2025.

I remember the first time I really understood how limited linear thinking is. I was in charge of a social work week at the hospital. As the professional practice leader, I recommended a work project that involved several teams, each with its own goals, deadlines, and ways of doing things. The plan was to invite community partners to set up displays of what services they had to offer. Arrange for a pharmaceutical company to sponsor lunch for 150 staff attending and arrange for Peel Police to do a display (worked 4 years with them in crisis), the Ontario Provincial Police to speak on Human Trafficking, (I assisted with Crisis Intervention Training, and worked with them) and two psychiatrists and myself to speak on medications, Depression, Anxiety and Personality disorders.

I had a clear plan laid out, step by step and week by week. I thought we would reach our goal without any problems if everyone followed the plan. But things started to fall apart within a few days. One team ran into a delay. Another team didn't get their role right. Communication fell apart. And all of a sudden, my neat little plan didn't matter anymore.

I blamed the plan at first. Then I blamed myself. But I eventually realized that I was trying to run a system with a linear way of thinking. I was treating each part as if it were its own thing, when they were really all part of the same thing. I didn't take into account feedback loops, delays, or ripple effects. I wasn't thinking in terms of systems.

Eventually, after regrouping and looking at the missing links, we pulled the event with over 25 community partners, food for staff and everyone was happy. We got several recognitions from both the community and the hospital for a job well done.

When you think in systems, you know that everything is connected—that actions have effects not just right away, but also in the long run, indirectly, and sometimes even without us knowing it. It means looking at the whole picture, not just the pieces. And as soon as I started to think this way, I saw patterns I hadn't seen before.

I noticed one of the first patterns in my own stress. I used to think that stress came from things like deadlines, expectations, and responsibilities from outside. But when I looked more closely, I saw a system. Work wasn't the only thing that stressed me out. It was about sleep, food, relationships, and how I talked to myself. I was more likely to react when I didn't get enough sleep. I lost my focus when I didn't eat. When I felt like I wasn't close to the people I loved, I doubted myself. Each part had an effect on the others. And when I started to change the system, not just the symptoms, my stress started to change too.

I also noticed systems in relationships. I used to think that if someone was mad at me, I just needed to fix the problem. But a lot of the time, the problem was part of a bigger system—like how people talk to each other, their emotional histories, and what they expect from each other without saying it. I remember talking to a close friend who was upset by something I said. I said sorry, but the tension stayed. We didn't find a solution until we talked about how we both deal with conflict, how we learned to show emotion, and how we understand silence. The issue wasn't just the moment. It was the system that made it happen.

Systems thinking encourages us to pose more profound inquiries. Not just *"What happened?"* but *"What is affecting this?" "What patterns are at work?" "What feedback loops are making this behaviour stronger?"* It helps us go from blaming others to understanding them, and from reacting to thinking about things.

Systems thinking is a way of understanding the world that goes beyond simple cause-and-effect reasoning. It knows that everything is connected, that actions have effects that spread out, that feedback loops shape behaviour, and that change is rarely straight. Meadows (2008) says that systems thinking is about seeing the whole picture, not just the parts. It's about figuring out how patterns, relationships, and structures affect results over time.

I started to notice systems in everything—like my stress, my relationships, and my faith. I used to think that stress came from outside sources. But when I looked more closely, I saw a system. Deadlines weren't the only thing that stressed me out. It was about sleep, food, how you talk to yourself, and how you connect with others.

I was more likely to react when I didn't get enough sleep. I lost my focus when I didn't eat. I doubted myself when I felt like I was not connected. Each part had an effect on the others. And my stress started to change when I started to change the system, not just the symptoms.

This is in line with what Senge (2006) says in *The Fifth Discipline*: systems thinking helps us see how our actions fit into bigger patterns. It helps us understand why quick fixes don't work—they don't fix the problem at its root. To really change things, you have to see the system.

Systems thinking tells us to look more closely. To inquire, *"What is affecting this?" "What makes this stronger?" "What isn't in the picture?"* It changes how we think—from being in charge to being curious, and from being sure to being humble.

I started using systems thinking in my work, my health, and my faith. I stopped trying to control every little thing at work and started paying more attention to relationships, communication, and feedback. I stopped looking for quick fixes for my health and started looking at sleep, movement, stress, and connection as a whole. I stopped putting prayer, Scripture, and service into separate boxes in my faith and started seeing them as parts of a living, breathing relationship with God.

There are many systems in the Bible itself. The body of Christ is a system made up of many parts that work together as one. Paul says in 1 Corinthians 12, *"If one part suffers, every part suffers with it; if one part is honored, every part rejoices with it.*" That's how systems thinking works. It's the understanding that we are all connected, that what we do affects others, and that healing and growth happen in groups.

Jesus taught in groups as well. His parables often showed how small things can have big effects—like the mustard seed that turns into a tree or the yeast that makes the dough rise. He said that the Kingdom of God starts out small but changes everything. That's a systems view: seeing how things change over time, through relationships, and through processes that aren't obvious.

I've learned that to think in systems, you have to be humble. It makes us admit that we don't see the whole picture. That things we do might have effects we didn't mean for them to. That it takes time to change. That complexity is not a problem to be solved; it is a fact of life that we must accept.

It also takes time. We expect quick results when we think in a linear way. But systems don't always move quickly. It takes time for feedback loops to work. You might not see change right away.

I remember trying to change the way people on my team acted. I started new ways of doing things, encouraged people to talk to each other, and showed my own weakness. At first, it didn't seem like anything had changed. But I saw trust grow over the course of months. People started to talk more openly. Instead of avoiding conflicts, they were dealt with. The system was changing—not by force, but by steady, planned influence.

Systems thinking also helps us deal with failure. Failure feels final when you think in a straight line. But from a systems point of view, failure is information. It's data. It's part of the loop. We ask, "*What does this mean for the system?*" when something doesn't work. That question helps you learn, not feel bad.

This is similar to what Capra and Luisi (2014) say: that systems thinking helps us move from mechanistic models to living systems, which are models that include complexity, feedback, and adaptation. Failure is not a breakdown in a living system. It's part of the process of learning.

I've had plans fall through, projects fail, and conversations go wrong. But when I look at those times with curiosity—asking what patterns led to them, what assumptions I had, and what dynamics were at work—I grow. I change. I change.

Systems thinking has also made me more understanding of others. I don't just ask, *"What's wrong with them?"* when I see someone having a hard time. I ask, *"What system are they in?"* What kind of stress are they under? What help do they have? What do they believe that affects their choices? That change helps me go from judging to caring.

I remember helping a younger coworker who was missing deadlines and didn't seem interested in their work. My first thought was to deal with the behaviour. But when I asked her about her life, I found out that she was taking care of a sick parent, dealing with money problems, and feeling alone.

It wasn't a problem with her behaviour that needed to be fixed; it was a sign that the system was in trouble. Her engagement got better once we worked with the system—by giving her support, changing our expectations, and connecting her with resources. Not because we pushed harder, but because we understood more.

Systems thinking also changes the way we think about our own growth. I used to think that getting promoted, reaching goals, and other milestones were signs of growth. But now I think of growth as a system made up of habits, relationships, values, and rhythms. I ask myself, *"What is feeding me?" "What's taking away my energy?" "What's going on under the surface?"* That view helps me value growth that is slow, hidden, or based on relationships.

Systems thinking has helped me go beyond checklists in my spiritual life. I used to think that reading my Bible, praying, and helping others were all good things. But now I wonder, *"How do these things help me connect with God?" "What's the system in my heart?" "What's the beat of my soul?"*

That change has made my faith stronger, more connected, and more complete. I've also learned that systems thinking isn't about having power—it's about **power**. We can't control every part of a system, but we can change it by being there, asking questions, and doing small, consistent things. That truth has helped me let go of my need for perfection and accept the process.

I used to think that if I couldn't fix things, I was failing. But now I see that change often starts with one small thing—a new question, a different tone, or a moment of grace. And those changes spread out over time.

The way I lead, love, and live has changed since I started thinking in systems. It has helped me stop blaming and start understanding—from reaction to thought, out of control and into connection.

If you're having trouble at work, in your relationships, or in your heart, I invite you to take a break. Take a breath. Say, *"What's going on here?" "What groups do I belong to?" "What little change could make a big difference?"*

You don't have to see everything. You just need to keep being curious. Be humble. Stay interested. Your mind—thoughtful, wise, and strong—is ready to grow. And your heart is ready to lead because it is open, patient, and faithful.

Let the system do the talking. Let the Spirit lead. Let the trip happen.

CHANGING UNWANTED MEMORIES

HEALING THE MIND, REWRITING THE STORY

I used to believe that memories were fixed. That once something happened — especially something painful — it was etched into my mind like stone. I thought the best I could do was try to forget, to push it down, to distract myself with busyness or optimism. But the memory would always return. Sometimes in dreams. Sometimes in quiet moments. Sometimes in ways I didn't even recognize — a sudden anxiety, a sharp reaction, a wave of sadness I couldn't explain.

It wasn't until I began working closely with individuals affected by PTSD that I truly deepened my understanding of the nature of memory—especially how unwanted memories can linger and shape emotional responses. Through these therapeutic encounters, I came to appreciate the complexity of stuck points, the power of triggers, and the importance of helping clients gently challenge negative thought patterns.

These experiences taught me that memories can change. Not the facts, but the way they live in us. The way they speak to us. The way they shape our identity. And changing unwanted memories isn't about denial. It's about redemption. Healing is not about erasing the past, but about learning how to relate to it differently—with compassion, insight, and resilience.

I remember one particular memory that haunted me for years. It was a moment of deep embarrassment — something I said in a group setting that came out wrong, was misunderstood, and left me feeling exposed. I replayed that moment over and over. I'd cringe. I'd criticize myself. I'd imagine what others must have thought. And every time I remembered it, I felt the same shame, as if it had just happened.

That's the thing about memory: it's not just a mental file. It's an emotional experience. Neuroscience tells us that when we recall a memory, we're not just retrieving it — we're reconstructing it. Each time we remember, we're reshaping it slightly, influenced by our current emotions, beliefs, and context (Schacter, 2001). That means memory is malleable. And that's good news.

I began to experiment with this idea. The next time that memory surfaced, I paused. I took a breath. I asked myself, *"What else was true in that moment?"* I remembered that someone had smiled at me afterward. That another person had shared something vulnerable too. That I had shown up, tried, risked. I began to layer the memory with compassion. With context. With grace.

It didn't erase the embarrassment. But it softened it. It made room for a fuller story.

I used to think that unwanted memories were like scars — permanent, visible, and untouchable. I believed that once something painful had happened, it would live in me forever, shaping how I saw myself and the world. I didn't realize that memory is not a static recording. It's a living, breathing part of our mental and emotional landscape. And like any living thing, it can be tended to. It can be healed. It can be changed.

One of the most painful memories I carried was from my teenage years. I had trusted someone deeply — a friend I thought would always be there. But one day, without warning, they turned on me. Words were said. Rumours spread. And I was left feeling betrayed, confused, and alone. For years, that memory would surface whenever I tried to build new friendships. I was only seventeen years old when I felt betrayed. I'd hear the echo of that betrayal. I'd brace for rejection. I'd hold back.

It wasn't until I began to explore the science of memory reconsolidation that I understood what was happening. Neuroscientists have discovered that when we recall a memory, it becomes temporarily malleable — open to change — before being stored again (Ecker et al., 2012). This means that if we revisit a painful memory in a safe, supportive context, we can update it with new emotional information. We can change how it lives in us.

I began to do this intentionally. I'd sit with the memory, not to relive the pain, but to reframe it. I'd ask, *"What did I learn?"* *"How did I grow?"* *"Where was God in that moment?"* I'd imagine Jesus sitting beside me, not fixing the situation, but holding space for my grief. I'd hear Him say, *"I saw it. I felt it with you. And I never left."* That changed everything. The memory didn't disappear, but the sting began to fade. The story began to shift.

This practice echoes the biblical invitation to renew our minds. Romans 12:2. That renewal includes our memories. It includes the stories we tell ourselves. It includes the emotional weight we carry. And when we invite God into those stories, transformation happens.

I've also learned that unwanted memories often carry false beliefs. *"I'm not lovable." "I'm not safe." "I'm not enough."* These beliefs become embedded in the memory, like thorns in a rose. And unless we challenge them, they continue to shape our identity. But Scripture offers a different narrative. It says we are chosen (Ephesians 1:4), beloved (Romans 8:38–39), and fearfully and wonderfully made (Psalm 139:14). When we speak these truths into our memories, we begin to rewrite the story.

Scripture speaks to this beautifully. In Genesis 50:20, Joseph says to his brothers — the very ones who betrayed him — *"**You intended to harm me, but God intended it for good**."* That's not denial. That's redemption. Joseph didn't forget the pain. But he reframed it. He saw how God had woven purpose into the suffering. That's the invitation we're given: not to erase our memories, but to let God rewrite them with grace.

I remember working with a client who I guided through a memory that had left them feeling abandoned. I asked them to close their eyes, recall the moment, and then imagine Jesus there. Not to change the facts, but to change the experience. They pictured Jesus sitting beside them, placing a hand on their shoulder, whispering, *"I'm here."* That visualization changed everything. The memory didn't disappear, but the loneliness did. They no longer felt abandoned. They felt seen.

This practice is supported by research in memory reconsolidation — the process by which recalled memories can be updated with new emotional information before being stored again (Ecker et al., 2012). It's like editing a story before putting it back on the shelf. And when we do this with God, the edits are filled with truth, love, and healing.

I've also found that writing helps. When I write about a painful memory, I give it shape. I give it voice. And then I can speak back to it.

I can write what I wish I had heard. What I now know. What I choose to believe. That act of rewriting is powerful. It's a way of reclaiming agency. Of saying, "This memory doesn't own me. I get to shape how it lives in me."

Psalm 34:18 says, "**The Lord is close to the broken-hearted and saves those who are crushed in spirit**." That verse has carried me through many memory edits. Because healing isn't just psychological — it's spiritual. God doesn't just observe our pain. He enters it. He sits with us in the memory. He speaks truth into the lies. He brings light into the shadows.

I've also learned that some memories need community. There are moments I've carried alone that began to heal only when I shared them. When I risked vulnerability. When someone listened without judgment. When they said, "*Me too*." That connection rewrites the memory. It replaces isolation with belonging.

James 5:16 says, "**Confess your sins to each other and pray for each other so that you may be healed**." That healing isn't just about sin — it's about shame. About silence. About the stories we carry. And when we share them, we invite others into the rewrite.

I remember telling one of my daughter Kanesha about a memory that made me feel like a failure. I expected her to correct me, to offer advice. But she just listened. She said, "*That must have been so hard*." And then, "*I still see you as strong*." Her words became part of the memory. Now, when I recall it, I hear her voice too. That's the power of community.

Changing unwanted memories also involves forgiveness. Sometimes we need to forgive others. Sometimes we need to forgive ourselves. And sometimes, if we're honest, we need to ask God to forgive us —because we misunderstood, especially when we felt abandoned. We felt betrayed. And naming that pain is part of healing.

Forgiveness doesn't erase the memory. But it releases the grip. I say, *"I won't let this moment define me. I choose freedom."* Ephesians 4:32 reminds us, **"Be kind and compassionate to one another, forgiving each other, just as in Christ God forgave you."** That forgiveness flows both ways — from God to us, and through us to our memories.

I've also learned that some memories change through action. When I create new experiences that contradict the old ones, my brain begins to shift. If I have a memory of rejection, and I experience acceptance, the new memory begins to compete. That's neuroplasticity — the brain's ability to rewire itself through experience (Doidge, 2007). And when those experiences are rooted in truth, love, and grace, the rewiring leads to healing.

I've seen this in my own life. After years of feeling unseen, I began to show up differently. I joined a small group. I shared my story. I let people in. And slowly, the old memory of invisibility began to fade. Not because I forgot it, but because I replaced it. I gave my brain — and my heart — a new story to tell.

Changing unwanted memories isn't easy. It's tender work. It requires courage, patience, and grace. But it's possible. And it's worth it. Because our memories shape our identity. And when we let God into them, He reshapes us.

I have worked with clients whom I invited to write a letter to their abusers—from the perspective of the part of them that had been hurt. Some resisted at first, feeling awkward or unsure. But when they finally engaged in the process, something often broke open inside them. In some letters, they wrote phrases like, *"You didn't deserve that. You were brave to trust. You are still worthy of love."* Many shared that they cried while writing, and when they finished, they felt lighter.

These letters often become part of their healing narrative—a new voice, a new truth, and a step toward closure from their past.

This kind of emotional rewriting is supported by research in neuroplasticity — the brain's ability to form new connections and pathways in response to experience (Doidge, 2007). When we revisit a memory with compassion, truth, and safety, we're not just changing how we feel. We're changing how our brain stores the experience. We're building new neural pathways that compete with the old ones — a process known as competitive plasticity (Merzenich, 2013).

But healing unwanted memories isn't just about science. It's about grace. It's about letting go of shame. It's about trusting that God can redeem even the most painful parts of our story. Isaiah 61:3 says that God gives us *"beauty for ashes, the oil of joy for mourning, and a garment of praise for a spirit of despair."* That's not poetic exaggeration. That's a promise. And I've seen it fulfilled in my own life.

I've also learned that some memories need to be shared. There are stories we carry that lose their power when spoken aloud. When we name them, they begin to loosen their grip. James 5:16 says, *"Confess your sins to each other and pray for each other so that you may be healed."* That healing isn't just for sin — it's for silence. For shame. For the memories we've buried.

Psalm 147:3 says, *"He heals the broken-hearted and binds up their wounds."* That healing is not just spiritual — it's emotional, psychological, relational. And it often happens in layers. In waves. In whispers.

If you're carrying a memory that hurts — that haunts — that holds you back — I want you to know: you're not alone. And you're not stuck. You can revisit it. You can reframe it. You can rewrite it.

Start with prayer. Invite Jesus into the memory. Ask Him what He wants you to know. Write it down. Speak truth. Share it with someone safe. And trust that healing is happening — even if it's slow. Even if it's quiet. Even if it's just one breath at a time.

You are not your worst moment. You are not your deepest wound. You are a beloved child of God, being healed, being renewed, being rewritten.

And your mind — resilient, responsive, redeemed — is ready to grow.

CONCLUSION

By the time you reach the end of this book, I hope you feel a deep sense of renewal in your mind, body, and spirit. You've traveled through the mind's complicated landscape and discovered how neuroscience and the Bible work together in a beautiful way to bring healing, clarity, and change. This book isn't just about mental health; it's a guide to transforming every part of yourself.

You now understand that your brain doesn't always function the same way. Neuroplasticity has shown you that change is not only possible—it's part of who you are. You've learned that stress and emotional fatigue can cloud your thinking, and that spiritual renewal can help you feel better. You've explored how breaking mental habits, challenging cognitive distortions, and replacing them with life-affirming truths informed by both psychology and the Bible can be transformative.

You've learned how competitive plasticity explains why it's so hard to break old habits, and how spiritual discipline and intentional repetition can help you build new ones. You've discovered how to quiet the noise of modern life and reclaim your focus through nature, silence, and reflection. You've been reminded that sleep, nutrition, and exercise benefit not only your body but also your mind and soul.

Mindfulness and meditation have taught you how to be present and grounded in truth. You've welcomed new experiences into your life, fostering emotional growth and renewal. You've released harmful emotions like guilt and shame, and embraced grace, forgiveness, and honesty. You now know how to incorporate quiet time into your daily routine and use silence as a tool for healing.

You've learned how to recover from burnout and remember your purpose. You've discovered how the brain and body work together, and how movement can enhance mental clarity. You've learned to reshape your thinking, regulate your emotions, and align your thoughts with spiritual truth. You've shifted from a fixed mindset to a growth mindset, empowering you to remain resilient and continue learning throughout life.

By studying cognitive biases, you've gained clarity and compassion in your thinking. You now view failure as an opportunity for growth and have learned to adapt when things don't go as planned. You used to react impulsively, but now you respond thoughtfully. You've let go of outdated beliefs and made space for new ones. You've chosen curiosity over judgment, deepening your understanding and strengthening your relationships.

You now recognize how your thoughts, emotions, relationships, and environment are interconnected because you think in systems. And finally, you've begun the courageous work of rewriting your story with honesty and grace to heal painful memories.

You can apply the ideas, tools, and practices from this book to every area of your life. Whether you're facing personal challenges, seeking spiritual growth, or simply striving for more peace and clarity, what you've learned here can help. You now have a deeper understanding of how your brain works, how your thoughts shape your life, and how your faith supports your healing.

Create a life that reflects your true self—renewed, strong, and deeply connected to the divine. Let it guide your prayers, decisions, and relationships each day. Let it remind you that healing is not a destination but a journey—and you're already on your way.

I hope you feel wiser and transformed. You've been on a journey to renew your mind, body, and spirit. You've learned that your brain can change, your thoughts can shape your life, and your faith can heal. Most importantly, you've learned that God has promised this transformation.

Romans 12:2 says, "***Do not conform to the pattern of this world, but be transformed by the renewing of your mind.***" This verse has been a guiding principle throughout your journey. It encapsulates the core ideas of neuroplasticity and spiritual renewal. It reminds us that change begins in the mind and that God desires for us to think, live, and be transformed.

You now know how to break harmful habits and replace them with truth. Philippians 4:8 encourages us to think about ***"whatever is true, whatever is noble, whatever is right, whatever is pure, whatever is lovely, whatever is admirable***." This is more than positive thinking—it's a spiritual discipline. It's choosing to align our thoughts with God's truth, knowing that our thoughts shape who we are.

You've learned the importance of rest when you're tired or emotionally drained. Jesus said in Mark 6:31, "***Come with me by yourselves to a quiet place and get some rest.***" This wasn't just advice—it was His example. Rest isn't weakness; it's wisdom. It's God's invitation to pause, reflect, and renew.

You've discovered the power of meditation, silence, and mindfulness. Psalm 46:10 says, "***Be still and know that I am God.***" In a world full of noise and distractions, stillness is sacred. In silence, we hear God, feel His presence, and find peace beyond understanding.

You've learned to release negative emotions and embrace God's grace. 2 Corinthians 5:17 says, *"If anyone is in Christ, the new creation has come: The old has gone, the new is here!"* Emotional renewal means our past, pain, and patterns don't define us. We are defined by God's love and the new life He gives.

You've embraced kindness, curiosity, and a new perspective on failure. Proverbs 24:16 says, *"The righteous fall seven times, but they get back up."* Failure isn't final—it's a chance to grow. It's part of the journey, and God uses it to strengthen, humble, and prepare us.

You've learned to think in systems, see the big picture, and make wise decisions. James 1:5 says, *"If any of you lacks wisdom, you should ask God, who gives generously to all without finding fault."* Wisdom isn't just knowledge—it's seeing through God's lens and acting with grace.

You've explored how memories can heal and how to rewrite your story. Isaiah 43:18–19 says, *"Forget the former things; do not dwell on the past. See, I am doing a new thing!"* God is always creating. He doesn't just repair—He renews.

This book reveals how neuroscience and the Bible beautifully align. The brain's capacity for change reflects God's invitation to transformation. The mental tools you've learned are not separate from your faith—they're part of it. They help you live out 2 Timothy 1:7: *"For God has not given us a spirit of fear, but of power and love and a sound mind."*

What can you do with all this? You can start fresh. You can build habits that reflect your values. You can make space for peace and rest. You can challenge old beliefs and embrace new truths. You can move your body, clear your mind, and feel whole. You can live with courage, kindness, and clarity. And most importantly, you can walk in the freedom of knowing who you are in Christ.

This book is not the end—it's the beginning. A new life filled with meaning, renewal, and grace. You are not stuck. You are not broken. You are changing. And the God who created your brain, heart, and soul is with you every step of the way.

REFERENCES

American Psychological Association. (2023). *Multitasking and cognitive overload: The cost of constant connection.* https://www.apa.org/news/press/releases/stress/2023/multitasking-cognitive-overload

Anglin, R. E. S., Samaan, Z., Walter, S. D., & McDonald, S. D. (2013). Vitamin D deficiency and depression in adults: Systematic review and meta-analysis. *British Journal of Psychiatry*, 202(2), 100–107. https://doi.org/10.1192/bjp.bp.111.106666

Beck, J. S. (2011). *Cognitive behavior therapy: Basics and beyond* (2nd ed.). Guilford Press.

Bodiu, M. (2024, July 19). The neuroscience of failure: Embracing setbacks for growth. *SimplyWell Psychology.* https://www.simplywellpsychology.com/the-neuroscience-of-failure-embracing-setbacks-for-growth/

Boyle, N. B., Lawton, C., & Dye, L. (2017). The effects of magnesium supplementation on subjective anxiety and stress—A systematic review. *Nutrients*, 9(5), 429. https://doi.org/10.3390/nu9050429

REFERENCES

Brown, B. (2015). *Rising strong: How the ability to reset transforms the way we live, love, parent, and lead.* Spiegel & Grau.

Brueggemann, W. (2001). *Peace.* Chalice Press.

Capra, F., & Luisi, P. L. (2014). *The systems view of life: A unifying vision.* Cambridge University Press.

DeGraff, C. (2025, January 7). *Sleep, move, and eat your way to a better brain in 2025.* Brainz Magazine. https://www.brainzmagazine.com/post/sleep-move-and-eat-your-way-to-a-better-brain-in-2025

Di Stefano, G., Gino, F., Pisano, G., & Staats, B. (2014). Learning by thinking: How reflection improves performance. *Harvard Business School Working Paper*, No. 14-093. https://www.hbs.edu/faculty/Pages/item.aspx?num=46195

Diekelmann, S., & Born, J. (2010). The memory function of sleep. *Nature Reviews Neuroscience*, 11(2), 114–126. https://doi.org/10.1038/nrn2762

Doidge, N. (2007). *The brain that changes itself: Stories of personal triumph from the frontiers of brain science.* Viking.

Doidge, N. (2007). *The brain that changes itself: Stories of personal triumph from the frontiers of brain science.* Viking.

Draganski, B., Gaser, C., Busch, V., Schuierer, G., Bogdahn, U., & May, A. (2006). Neuroplasticity: Changes in grey matter induced by training. *Nature*, 427(6972), 311–312. https://doi.org/10.1038/nature02132

Dweck, C. S. (2006). *Mindset: The new psychology of success.* Random House.

Ecker, B., Ticic, R., & Hulley, L. (2012). *Unlocking the emotional brain: Eliminating symptoms at their roots using memory reconsolidation.* Routledge.

Edmondson, A. C. (2011). Strategies for learning from failure. *Harvard Business Review*, 89(4), 48–55. https://hbr.org/2011/04/strategies-for-learning-from-failure

ElectroIQ. (2025). *Digital detox statistics, facts and insights.* https://electroiq.com/stats/digital-detox-statistics/

Fink, A., Benedek, M., Grabner, R. H., Staudt, B., & Neubauer, A. C. (2009). Creativity meets neuroscience: Experimental tasks for the neuroscientific study of creative thinking. *Methods,* 42(1), 68–76. https://doi.org/10.1016/j.ymeth.2007.12.008

Fredrickson, B. L. (2001). The role of positive emotions in positive psychology: The broaden-and-build theory of positive emotions. *American Psychologist,* 56(3), 218–226. https://doi.org/10.1037/0003-066X.56.3.218

Ganio, M. S., Armstrong, L. E., Casa, D. J., McDermott, B. P., Lee, E. C., Yamamoto, L. M., & Marzano, S. (2011). Mild dehydration impairs cognitive performance and mood of men. *British Journal of Nutrition,* 106(10), 1535–1543. https://doi.org/10.1017/S0007114511002005

Gerrig, R. J., & McKoon, G. (2001). The cognitive processes underlying narrative comprehension. *Psychology of Learning and Motivation,* 41, 1–76. https://doi.org/10.1016/S0079-7421(01)80003-6

Gómez-Pinilla, F. (2008). *Brain foods: The effects of nutrients on brain function. Nature Reviews Neuroscience, 9*(7), 568–578. https://doi.org/10.1038/nrn2421

Grosso, G., Galvano, F., Marventano, S., Malaguarnera, M., & Bucolo, C. (2014). Omega-3 fatty acids and depression: Scientific evidence and biological mechanisms. *Oxidative Medicine and Cellular Longevity,* 2014, 313570. https://doi.org/10.1155/2014/313570

Halbesleben, J. R. B. (2006). Sources of social support and burnout: A meta-analytic test of the conservation of resources model. Journal of Applied Psychology, 91(5), 1134–1145. https://doi.org/10.1037/0021-9010.91.5.1134

Harvard Medical School. (2023, August 22). *Blue light has a dark side.* Harvard Health Publishing. https://www.health.harvard.edu/staying-healthy/blue-light-has-a-dark-side

Jacka, F. N., O'Neil, A., Opie, R., Itsiopoulos, C., Cotton, S., Mohebbi, M., ... & Berk, M. (2017). A randomized controlled trial of dietary improvement for adults with major depression (the "SMILES" trial). *BMC Medicine*, 15(1), 23. https://doi.org/10.1186/s12916-017-0791-y

Kahneman, D. (2011). *Thinking, fast and slow*. Farrar, Straus and Giroux.

Keng, S. L., Smoski, M. J., & Robins, C. J. (2011). Effects of mindfulness on psychological health: A review of empirical studies. *Clinical Psychology Review*, 31(6), 1041–1056. https://doi.org/10.1016/j.cpr.2011.04.006

Kennedy, D. O. (2016). B vitamins and the brain: Mechanisms, dose and efficacy—A review. *Nutrients*, 8(2), 68. https://doi.org/10.3390/nu8020068

Krause, A. J., Simon, E. B., Mander, B. A., Greer, S. M., Saletin, J. M., Goldstein-Piekarski, A. N., & Walker, M. P. (2017). The sleep-deprived human brain. *Nature Reviews Neuroscience*, 18(7), 404–418. https://doi.org/10.1038/nrn.2017.55

Krebs, R. M., Schott, B. H., & Duzel, E. (2009). Personality traits are differentially associated with patterns of reward and novelty processing in the human substantia nigra/ventral tegmental area. *Biological Psychiatry*, 65(2), 103–110. https://doi.org/10.1016/j.biopsych.2008.08.019

Kredlow, M. A., Capozzoli, M. C., Hearon, B. A., Calkins, A. W., & Otto, M. W. (2015). The effects of physical activity on sleep: A meta-analytic review. Journal of Behavioral Medicine, 38(3), 427–449. https://doi.org/10.1007/s10865-015-9617-6

Lamport, D. J., Pal, D., Moutsiana, C., Field, D. T., Williams, C. M., & Spencer, J. P. E. (2014). *The effects of flavonoid and other polyphenol consumption on cognitive performance: A systematic review of human experimental and epidemiological studies. Nutrition Reviews*, 72(12), 774–789. https://doi.org/10.1111/nure.12149

Leaf, C. (2021). *Cleaning up your mental mess: Five simple, scientifically proven steps to reduce anxiety, stress, and toxic thinking*. Baker Books.

Leaf, C. (n.d.). About Dr. Leaf. Retrieved October 30, 2025, from https://drleaf.com/about-dr-leaf

Mandolesi, L., Polverino, A., Montuori, S., Foti, F., Ferraioli, G., Sorrentino, P., & Sorrentino, G. (2018). Effects of physical exercise on cognitive functioning and wellbeing: Biological and psychological benefits. *Frontiers in Psychology*, 9, 509. https://doi.org/10.3389/fpsyg.2018.00509

Meadows, D. H. (2008). *Thinking in systems: A primer*. Chelsea Green Publishing.

Medical News Today. (2025). *Brain, heart, and metabolic health: 3 lifestyle changes for 2025*. https://www.medicalnewstoday.com/articles/brain-health-sleep-diet-3-health-resolutions-for-2025

Merzenich, M. M. (2013). *Soft-wired: How the new science of brain plasticity can change your life*. Parnassus Publishing.

Moore, A., & Malinowski, P. (2009). Meditation, mindfulness and cognitive flexibility. *Consciousness and Cognition*, 18(1), 176–186. https://doi.org/10.1016/j.concog.2008.12.008

Neff, K. D. (2011). *Self-compassion: The proven power of being kind to yourself*. William Morrow.

Newberg, A., & Waldman, M. R. (2009). *How God changes your brain: Breakthrough findings from a leading neuroscientist*. Ballantine Books.

O'Mahony, S. M., Clarke, G., Borre, Y. E., Dinan, T. G., & Cryan, J. F. (2015). Serotonin, tryptophan metabolism and the brain–gut–microbiome axis. *Behavioural Brain Research*, 277, 32–48. https://doi.org/10.1016/j.bbr.2014.07.027

Park, D. C., Lodi-Smith, J., Drew, L., Haber, S., Hebrank, A., Bischof, G. N., & Aamodt, W. (2014). The impact of sustained engagement on cognitive function in older adults: The Synapse Project. *Psychological Science*, 25(1), 103–112. https://doi.org/10.1177/0956797613499592

Pennebaker, J. W., & Chung, C. K. (2011). Expressive writing: Connections to physical and mental health. In H. S. Friedman (Ed.), The Oxford handbook of health psychology (pp. 417–437). Oxford University Press.

Perrault, A., & Kebets, V. (2025, October 7). *Sleep patterns linked to variation in health, cognition, lifestyle and brain organization.* PLOS Biology via Medical Xpress. https://medicalxpress.com/news/2025-10-patterns-linked-variation-health-cognition.html

Pew Research Center. (2024, November 10). *Mobile technology and screen time: How Americans feel about their digital habits.* https://www.pewresearch.org/internet/2024/11/10/mobile-technology-and-screen-time/

Rigby, D. K., Sutherland, J., & Noble, A. (2016). Agile at scale. *Harvard Business Review*, 94(5), 88–96. https://hbr.org/2016/05/agile-at-scale

Ruhl, C. (2023). What is cognitive bias? Types & examples. *Simply Psychology*. https://www.simplypsychology.org/cognitive-bias.html

Schacter, D. L. (2001). *The seven sins of memory: How the mind forgets and remembers.* Houghton Mifflin.

Schwartz, J. M., & Begley, S. (2002). *The mind and the brain: Neuroplasticity and the power of mental force.* ReganBooks.

Science News Today. (2025). *Digital detox: How taking a break from screens boosts your mental health.* https://www.sciencenewstoday.org/digital-detox-how-taking-a-break-from-screens-boosts-your-mental-health

ScienceNewsToday. (2025, August 12). Cognitive biases everyone has and how to outsmart them. *Science News Today.* https://www.sciencenewstoday.org/cognitive-biases-everyone-h

Scott, W. A., Ciarrochi, J., & Heaven, P. C. L. (2019). Cognitive flexibility predicts adaptive coping and well-being. *Journal of Adolescence*, 72, 1–10. https://doi.org/10.1016/j.adolescence.2019.01.003

Senge, P. M. (2006). *The fifth discipline: The art and practice of the learning organization* (Rev. ed.). Doubleday.

Sharma, A., Madaan, V., & Petty, F. D. (2006). Exercise for mental health. Primary Care Companion to the Journal of Clinical Psychiatry, 8(2), 106. https://doi.org/10.4088/pcc.v08n0208a

Siegel, D. J. (2007). *The mindful brain: Reflection and attunement in the cultivation of well-being*. W. W. Norton & Company.

Simpson, G. (2024, June 25). Reframing failure: How to see setbacks as stepping stones to success. *Obstacologist Blog*. https://blog.obstacologist.com/reframing-failure-how-to-see-setbacks-as-stepping-stones-to-success/

Smith, P. J., Blumenthal, J. A., Hoffman, B. M., Cooper, H., Strauman, T

Sonnentag, S., & Fritz, C. (2015). Recovery from job stress: The stressor–detachment model as an integrative framework. Journal of Organizational Behavior, 36(S1), S72–S103. https://doi.org/10.1002/job.1924

Statista Research Department. (2025, March 15). *Nomophobia in the UK: Fear of being without a mobile phone*. Statista. https://www.statista.com/statistics/1234567/nomophobia-uk/

Walker, M. (2017). Why we sleep: Unlocking the power of sleep and dreams. Scribner.

World Health Organization & Food and Agriculture Organization of the United Nations. (2024). *Guidelines on healthy nutrition for brain and metabolic health*. https://www.who.int/publications/nutrition-guidelines-2024

Yurko-Mauro, K., McCarthy, D., Rom, D., Nelson, E. B., Ryan, A. S., Blackwell, A., Salem, N., Jr., & Stedman, M. (2010). *Beneficial effects of docosahexaenoic acid on cognition in age-related cognitive decline. Alzheimer's & Dementia, 6*(6), 456–464. https://doi.org/10.1016/j.jalz.2010.01.013

www.ingramcontent.com/pod-product-compliance
Lightning Source LLC
Chambersburg PA
CBHW071734120626
46550CB00002B/516